FROM A STORM TO A HURRICANE

Rory Storm
&
The Hurricanes

ANTHONY HOGAN

AMBERLEY

This book is dedicated to Alan, Rory, John, Johnny, Charles, Ty, Walter, Lou, Richard, Ringo, Jimmy Tushingham, Reg Hales, Jim Turner, John Carter, Spud Ward, Jeff Truman, Paul Murphy, Roy Rich, Derek Fell, Bobby Thomson, Vicki Woods, Anthony Ashdown, Gibson Kemp, Brian Johnson, Keith Hartley, Ian Broad, Trevor Morais, Vince Earl, Dave May, Karl Terry, Carl Rich, Keith Alcock, Adrian Lord and all those who filled in with the band under its many different names. With thanks for what they gave us.

Author's note: Some of the images in this book are of poor quality, but they are of great value to the story and so have been included.

First published 2016

Amberley Publishing
The Hill, Stroud
Gloucestershire, GL5 4EP

www.amberley-books.com

Copyright © Anthony Hogan, 2016

The right of Anthony Hogan to be identified as the Author of this work has been asserted in accordance with the Copyrights, Designs and Patents Act 1988.

British Library Cataloguing in Publication Data.
A catalogue record for this book is available from the British Library.

ISBN 978 1 4456 5632 8 (print)
ISBN 978 1 4456 5633 5 (ebook)

Map and table design by Thomas Bohm, User design.
Typesetting and Origination by Amberley Publishing.
Printed in the UK.

Contents

Foreword by Iris Caldwell

As children, he used to tease and aggravate me. He'd put Daddy Long Legs in my bed and chase me with worms! He even put me in the bin once. He made me laugh and he made me mad. He beat me at everything except bedtime; when I didn't want to go to bed, he'd say, 'Come on, I'll race you to morning.' I'd run upstairs and jump into bed and squeeze my eyes tight until I fell asleep. He wasn't a morning person so I beat him every day until that last morning when all races ended.

He is my friend, my hero and my big, handsome, talented and oh so loving brother. I pray that he knows how very much I love him and I wish I could 'race him to morning' just one more time. He was our mum's (Ma Storm) and our dad's Mr Showmanship. With his gold lamé jackets and signature blonde quiff, teenage girls would scream for him. Mersey Beat would have been poorer without him and his band of brothers – The Hurricanes – Johnny Guitar, Ty, Lou and Ringo, not forgetting Jimmy Tush and others you'll read about in the following pages (the best band on the scene, in my opinion). From Butlins to Beatles, Hamburg to Huyton, with hurdles to conquer, both artiste and athlete, he raced through life. How lucky was I to have been a part of such a family.

Bless you all who remember those lads and the joy they gave, and especially that Golden Boy with the infectious smile who gave so much of himself, and bless those who still hold them in their heart. And thank you to Ant, who has taken so much time and effort to capture their lives and personalities in this book. His name was Rory and music was his story.

Iris (Rory's little sister)

1

From Little Acorns

Ernest Caldwell was born Ernest George Waddington Caldwell on 20 June 1908 in Liverpool, to Samuel George Caldwell and Margaret Alice Waddington. He spent his early years living at No. 59 Leinster Road in the Old Swan area of the city. His father had been born in Portaferry, County Down in Ireland, and was employed as a shop assistant selling clothing. Ernest's mother and his siblings were all born in Liverpool. In the early 1930s, Ernest was employed as a clerk at the Automatic Telephone and Electric Co. in Edge Lane. His life was basically planned out: work hard, gain promotion, and secure a future at the company.

While at work he noticed Violet Disley, and secretly held a crush for her. He was far too shy to ask her out on a date, fearing the shame of rejection, so he admired her from afar. What else could he do? His heart longed for her as he watched her at work, but his courage was not strong enough to approach her. A friend of Violet's informed Ernest that she was also keen on him and egged him on to ask her out. He plucked up the courage and decided he would do it, but as he approached her he lost his nerve. Ernest then burst into song and sang 'Come to me Violetta'. Violet was impressed, laughed, and agreed to the date.

Violet was born Violet Disley on 24 July 1908 in Liverpool, to Richard Disley, born 1847 in Berrie, Mid Wales, an electrical labourer for the Liverpool corporation (he had also worked as a cobbler) and Alice Turner, born 1871 in Rock Ferry, Cheshire, who worked as a cleaner and took in washing. Violet grew up at No. 7 Childers Street, Old Swan, doting after her little brother Len who she loved so much. Unlike Ernie she was very talkative, loved dancing, and to dream a life that she saw in the movies. After meeting Ernie at work they began to date. Ernie was happy to dance with her and take her to the Curzon cinema. They were the complete opposite of one another, but it worked for them. It was soon clear that they were both deeply in love, and wedding bells rang on 11 April 1936, when the couple married at St Anne's church, Stanley.

Ernie and Vi on their wedding day. (Courtesy of Iris Caldwell)

They both gave their address as No. 7 Childers street on the marriage certificate. At first they rented a small flat above a greengrocers store by the Rocket on Queens Drive. Vi's sister Doris was a worker at the store. They then found a house at No. 54 Broad Green Road, a short walk from the shopping area of Old Swan in Liverpool. The house had three bedrooms, a bathroom with an inside toilet, and a large back garden; a perfect place to raise a family.

Violet become pregnant with their first child, Alan Ernest Caldwell, who was born in the front bedroom of their home on 7 January 1938. Vi and Ernie were filled to the brim with joy at his arrival. Len Disley, Violet's younger brother, was keen to see his nephew and visited with a gift of a fire engine. Maybe not the best toy to give to a new born baby? But it shows that his heart and excitement was there. The family settled into their new life feeling happy and secure, and then the world went crazy.

Britain had entered the Second World War on 3 September 1939 when it declared war on Germany. Liverpool, being a major port city, was a target for the Luftwaffe, with the bombing raids in this region starting in August 1940. When the sirens sounded, Vi would take Alan into the shelter that stood just after the Gardeners Arms public house, a two-minute walk from their home. If Ernie was not at his work or out helping those caught up in the bombings, he would accompany them. The shelter (Known as the Rocket Shelter) was an 'E Type Shelter' built in the shape of the letter E and also underground, so as to give extra protection. Vi would try to comfort little Alan as the bombs fell and the terrific sounds of explosions resounded into the shelter, along with the noise of the nearby 'Ack Ack' guns as they opened up on the enemy above. It was horrific, but the worst was still to come. The Christmas blitz of 1940 was particularly heavy, yet Violet still refused to be evacuated from her city with Alan.

The family had a small shelter in their garden that they could also use. The 'Anderson Shelter', as it was known, came free to those who earned less than £5 per week. Ernie received one free, but had to construct it himself. Two curved corrugated-steel panels were used to cover a hole dug into the ground. It proved to be a simple yet effective idea. Ernest also had to sign the official secrets act at his work, when they were ordered to make navigation equipment for the Royal Air Force.

Violet had the constant worry of her brother Len, who was by this time serving with the Royal Army Medical Corps as a driver with the service number T/100624. By May 1941, Vi would have more to worry about as the Germans decided to hit Liverpool as hard as they could. The first two nights of May had brought bombing to many areas of the city; it was clear to all that it was far from over. Then came to the night of 3/4 May 1941, a night the city would never forget.

When the sirens rang out on the evening of 3 May, people made their way to the shelters. A nearby dance hall had been evacuated

Alan pictured outside the Anderson shelter in the back garden of No. 54 Broad Green Road. (Courtesy of Iris Caldwell)

and most of the people went into the Rocket shelter. Ernie, Violet and Alan had decided to use the Anderson shelter in their own back garden that night; their decision not to go to the Rocket Shelter saved their lives as that shelter took a direct hit in the raid. At least twenty-nine people were killed, with many more injured. Fred Disley, a private with the Royal Army Pay Corps, was killed in the shelter. It is uncertain if he was a relative of Violet, but it is possible that he was her cousin.

Ernie's good friend and work colleague Tom Thomasen was living in nearby Statton Road. On the night of the bombing he had taken his family into the Rocket shelter. Tom, his wife Matilda, and their children Thomas, twelve, Marjorie, eight, Ivy, seven, and Andrea, six, were all killed when the bomb hit. Ernie was devastated by the loss of this family and the horror that had reached his city. He resigned from his job at the Automatic Telephone & Electric Co. the following morning.

The huge raids continued each night until 8 May. The attacks then slackened off, leaving Liverpool wounded and in sorrow but undefeated. As the year passed by, the raids became less and less. Christmas was nearing and Ernie and Vi were trying to make it a treat for Alan. It was all about to be ruined however. Violet received the dreadful news that her beloved brother Len had died at war. He had been fighting at Tobruk in Libya, and was injured when the vehicle he was travelling in hit a landmine. He was taken to hospital where his legs were put in plaster. Len was then placed aboard a Red Cross ship that set sail with many other injured men. The ship was clearly marked with the Red Cross colours, yet it was spotted and attacked by an Italian Frigate on 5 December 1941. The ship was sunk, with many men lost, Len included; he was just twenty-five. His name was later added to the Alamein Memorial in Egypt. When the ship was hit, Len's friend had tried to pick him up and save him, but Len told him, 'Leave me here, save yourself, I cannot move in plaster.' The death of her brother hit violet hard. It could also be one of the reasons for what would happen to her a few years later. The raids died down, and by early 1942 they were gone forever. The scars however still remained.

The family tried to live as normal a life as possible. Ernest had left his job and taken a gamble on becoming a window cleaner. He bought all he needed – ladder, buckets, etc, – before looking for clients. It worked, and he soon had a large round that was bringing in enough money to keep the family. Throughout this period we can also get a sense of the kindness of this 'mild-mannered' man, as Ernie began to take notice of people's situations during his work. If he saw a home with no fire burning during the cold months he would later return to leave a bag of coal on the doorstep. He would often set out early for work, giving himself enough time to clean the windows free of charge for many who could not afford to pay. He would also give his time to a number of charities, and even sent crates of oranges to Russia when he heard that people were starving there.

After all the heartache and horror encountered during the war, some happiness returned to the family on 6 March 1944 when their daughter Iris was born. By this time it was also clear that young Alan had a bad speech impediment. At first, the family doctor tried to help Alan. He was then sent to have hypnosis therapy, but it failed to help him control his stammer. A stutter back in those days was not looked upon kindly, with those who stammered being classed as stupid. He also had a new hobby – fire. He would light fires on the bombed areas that he played on, then wait until the firemen arrived to put the fire out, fascinated as he watched them. Alan attended Broad Green Infants and Juniors school. He liked it, but struggled with his speech.

Although his stammer was rather severe, Alan would not let it hold him back. He loved playing out, was full of energy, and had turned into a practical joker, telling one teacher who asked him his name that it was 'Alan Cornflake' as it was easier for him to say than Caldwell. A close friend to Alan in his early childhood was his classmate Dennis,

All Saint's Church on Broad Green Road. Ernie was a regular here, and Alan and Iris also attended this church.

the two always being together. Ernie turned the Anderson shelter in the back garden into a den for the boys, and here they would play their imaginary games.

The war had changed people, and the Caldwells were no exception. Ernie had turned to the Bible in an attempt to find some comfort from what he had witnessed during the bombing raids. He would regularly attend All Saints Church along Broad Green Road, though Vi refused to go with him – she had no time for religion after the war years. Vi devoted herself to the children, they were her saviour from the heartache that she felt for her brother, and their friends who had died. Was Alan's stutter a result of the bombing raids that he experienced? Was it from the sorrow he saw in his mother and father? We will never know the answer, but it is possible that the war had caused in whole, or part, his speech defect. His stammer frustrated Alan, who just wanted to be like all the other kids. Vi was always boosting his confidence, telling him that he could do anything he wanted to do and that no stutter could stop him.

Life had to go on after the war, and people began to get back into some kind of routine. Vi and Ernie would take the kids to the local cinemas, the Carlton and the Curzon, with summer family holidays being enjoyed at Pwllheli in Wales. Ernie and Vi never drank, and lived their lives for their children, though a lot of their social events took place in the Old Swan/ White House pub or at the Gardeners Arms. In 1946, the football league made its return and Alan asked his father to take him to watch Liverpool play. Ernie asked him if he was sure that he did not want to go and watch Everton instead, but Alan was adamant, it had to be Liverpool. The kids in school had all been talking about Liverpool striker Albert Stubbins, and he wanted to go and see him.

Ernie bought tickets for the boy's pen in the Kop and took Alan to his first match on 7 April 1947, for a match against Preston North End. Alan was too small to see anything, but he was caught up in the atmosphere of the 46,000-strong crowd. He heard the cheering of the goals and the singing of the players' and teams' name. He sang along with no hint of his stammer and it felt good; he had a voice like everyone else. Liverpool ran out 3-0 winners with Albert Stubbins scoring two of the goals. He became Alan's hero, and Alan was ecstatic when the team went on to win the league in that same season. Incidentally, playing for Preston North End that day was a certain Bill Shankly, the future manager of Liverpool FC. Alan started attending most of their home games, and funnily enough Albert Stubbins would later appear on the cover of The Beatles 'Sergeant Pepper's Lonely Hearts Club Band' album.

Alan and Iris both started dancing lessons, with their parents being keen to back them in anything they wanted to do. First they danced at Winnie Mac's (Winifred McNally) tap dancing school opposite their home at No. 167 Broad Green road that was run by their mother Violet's

Alan as a baby in the family home. (Courtesy of Iris Caldwell)

friend Winnie. Later they joined the Billy Martin School of Dance situated on nearby Derby Lane, known as 'Martin's Dance Centre'. They were both pretty good at dancing, with Iris showing a notable skill. She would dance at the Curzon Cinema in Old Swan during the intervals, thrilling the public with her talent. Alan had also taken part in a number of local pantomimes and plays as a young boy. He and his sister were made for the limelight. A newspaper advert from that time reads, 'TEACHER OF DANCING: Broad Green School of Dancing (Miss Winnie Mac, M.B.A.T.D., M.A.D.A. Principal) 167 Broad Green rd 13.'

Ernie could be seen riding around the area on his bicycle, collecting old newspapers, magazines, and books from the local houses. These he would take to the St Vincent's hospice for the dying on Broad Green Road, where he would hand them out, along with sweets, to the residents. He was also known to spend time reading and chatting to many of them, a truly kind act from a very caring man. Ernie took another job as a porter in nearby Broadgreen Hospital. Here, he was known for his cheerful ways, and brought many a laugh to the patients by singing to them.

At Christmas time, Ernie would dress as Father Christmas and fill a pillow slip with twopenny Dairy Milk bars that he would hand out to the residents at St Vincent's. Alan and Iris would go along with him, with Alan dressed in a top hat singing 'Silent Night' and 'Once in Royal David's City' before the whole family sang carols. On Boxing Day Ernie would visit again, with the residents telling him all about Santa and the two children who had entertained them. They had no idea it had been Ernie.

Alan's and Iris's friends were always welcomed by Ernie and Vi. They had a long shed on the path at the side of the house that was made from the corrugated iron of their old Second World War Anderson shelter that the children would play in. At Halloween, Iris and her friends would hold shows there, with any money collected being used to buy fireworks and potatoes for the bonfire on Guy Fawkes night. On several occasions, Alan would be sitting in waiting at the back of the shed dressed as a ghost, ready to jump up and scare the girls. Vi had a wonderful way with children and always had an endless supply of games to play with them. The children also used the shed as a ghost train, putting paving slabs on bricks as a track, hanging cotton as cobwebs, and using the kettle whistle for the train. Alan of course would be hiding, covered in a sheet ready to jump out. A truly happy home, and delight for any child who visited. Iris was terrified of the daddy-long-legs insects, so Alan would collect lots of them from the garden and carefully place them in her bed with the sheet over them, so that when she went to bed and pulled back the sheet they would all fly up and scare her. He also once put her in the steel dustbin and put the lid on. Iris still has the scar on her leg that she received in that adventure.

Alan started school at the Highfield Secondary Modern in Broad Green. He had no interest when they suggested that he should try out for the school orchestra, and was less than impressed when they asked him to sing the George Formby hit 'When I'm Cleaning Windows' as he thought it would be an insult to his father who was a window cleaner. He decided to try out for the athletics team instead.

Once he started to run, everyone sat up and took notice, for it was plain to see that he was a natural middle-distance runner. Alan was snapped up by a neighbour, Bob Cooke, for the Pembroke Harrier's Athletic club, with whom he trained and competed. Local newspapers quickly began reporting about the potential of the young runner named Alan Caldwell. He would go on to become a very good 3000-metre

Alan already a singing star at an early age. (Courtesy of Iris Caldwell)

Steeplechaser, recording a personal best time of 9.28 minutes. He also managed to record a time of 4 minutes and 7 seconds for the 1500 metres. His running was that good that he was later considered for training towards the 1960 Olympics in Rome.

A young Alan riding his bike. (Courtesy of Iris Caldwell)

He was training six days a week with his coach Walter Thompson at the Athletic ground in Long Lane, Fazakerley, and on 22 January 1954 he became the club champion of the Pembroke Harrier's – his first trophy had been won. On 10 December 1955, Alan broke the club's 3-mile record at Southport while still an Under 20 competitor, with a time of 16 minutes 31 seconds. In the 1956 Waterloo Road Race, Alan could be seen cruising past the other competitors in the latter stages. To the annoyance of some he was singing 'Rock Around The Clock' very loudly as he ran to victory. Many trophies came his way as his obvious talent shone through, and all were displayed with pride in the family home.

In 1954, Roy Rogers came to Liverpool. He rode Trigger through the streets to The Empire theatre, with hundreds of people walking alongside them and others waiting in Lime Street. Alan was one of those walking along with his heroes. Vi had given him money to buy a ticket for Roy Rogers' show at the Empire theatre. Alan saw that tickets were still on sale, but that they cost a lot more than his mother had given him. Not wanting to embarrass her as he knew that money was tight, he gave her the money back when he returned home and told her that the tickets had all been sold.

Just before Christmas 1954, Alan and his uncle Eric jumped the train to Birmingham; Alan was off to watch his first Liverpool FC away game. Oh! the excitement, oh! the pride, oh! the passion, oh! the score ... Birmingham won 9-1. Alan was fuming. Cold, hungry, and angry he made his way back on the train. Arriving home he had something to eat and a cup of tea, then made his way to bed. He struggled to sleep. The worry had set in, and all he could think was 'those bloody Evertonians and their Dixie Dean are going to rip me apart, 9 bloody 1'.

Alan was sent for speech therapy with a Mr Good. He was growing near manhood and his speech difficulties were a huge frustration to him. He was very good looking, with girls showing him a lot of attention, yet he was painfully shy around them due to his stammer. Mr Good tried his best, but nothing succeeded. During one session Alan was given an injection that left him groggy. He returned home by bus, and as he was getting off he stumbled and sprained his ankle. A few days later he went with the scouts to Lake Windermere, where he performed his 12.5-mile outer-length swim of the lake. No sprained ankle could hold him back – truly amazing. Alan found his stammer a curse; it brought him unwanted attention, with some people making him the figure of fun. But he rose above it and used his crazy antics and sporting talents to become popular. He craved the limelight, in fact he loved it. His sporting achievements gave him a sense of pride and importance that his stammer would never allow him. To see himself in the local papers made him feel like a star, and he liked it.

The athletics for Alan, and the dancing lessons for Iris, cost money, and cash had begun to become scarce for the family. Alan overheard his parents talking about their money troubles. Ernie would explain to Vi that the athletic trips and dancing were costing more than they could afford. She would shout at him that the kids were talented and that they needed to ensure that they allowed them to carry on. Ernie and Vi had tried to hide their money troubles from their children, but once Alan heard what was going on he was distraught that they were struggling, and was determined to help them.

Alan decided that he would leave school and find a job, so he could pay for a few things himself. He managed to get himself an interview at the Hannay Cotton Co. in Chapel Street. He was terrified about his interview because of his stammer, but he went along and managed to get the job. He hated working there, but it helped him pay for the athletics and dancing, and he could contribute to the family funds. Incidentally, while working at Hannay's one of Alan's co-workers was James McCartney, father of a boy named Paul, who would go on to become a Beatle.

Violet began to show a lot of stress. The loss of her brother Len and friends in the Second World War, her worry about Alan's stammer and the family money troubles all contributed. It all became too much for her and she suffered a mental breakdown. After seeing a psychiatrist she was admitted to hospital. Here, over five days, Vi received electrotherapy

Alan alongside some of his many athletic trophies. (Courtesy of Iris Caldwell)

(ECT). Vi was a lot better on her return home, but was tired and in pain. Ernie now stayed at home more to look after his wife. Alan took it upon himself to help the family as much as he could while his mother was ill. For a young lad this showed huge maturity, and also gives a sense of just how close this family was to each other.

At work Alan enjoyed the football banter with the other guys. Who is the best team? Liverpool or Everton? But the girls he still found hard to talk to, his stammer stopping the normal flirtations of youth. He was excited when told that a girl at his work liked him – he liked her as well. Her name was Phyllis and she was very attractive. At home he wondered what he should do. Should he ask her out? He decided that he would and bought cinema tickets. He then became terrified and ashamed of his stutter. Almost in panic he practiced what he would say to her in front of a mirror. Back at work the moment had come to ask her out. His stomach was turning and he could feel the sweat building on his body. They were alone, and he seized his chance. The words however, deserted him, with his stammer taking control. Phyllis looked on sympathetically as Alan tried to get out the words. He was so embarrassed that he walked away, vowing never to ask her again. He hated his stutter, why was it doing this to him?

Alan was a gifted sportsman, playing football as a winger due to his speed, and even managing to get himself a game with the Liverpool players at their Melwood training ground. He was a very strong swimmer, breaking an underwater record of 73 yards, and swimming the entire 12.5-mile outer length of Lake Windermere. He attended the Silver Blades Ice Skating Rink on Prescot Road in Kensington twice a week, where of course he was a natural skater, and he joined the ice hockey team there. He also played golf at Allerton golf course, taking to it well and causing a few stares from the regulars as he often played wearing shorts. The Pembroke Harriers were based at Court Hey back in the 1950s, around a mile from Alan's house. Road trail races were popular events and when the club held a local trail the competitors would turn at The Rocket at the bottom of Broad Green Road. Vi, the neighbours, Iris, and the local kids would all be waiting with banners, ready to cheer Alan on.

An old school friend of Alan's, Paul Murphy, lived close to him in Heliers Road. Paul told Alan that he had bought a guitar and was trying to learn to play it. He told him how he would listen to Fats Domino, Gene Vincent, Carl Perkins, Chuck Berry, and the other American musicians on the radio, and try to copy the music on his instrument. Alan had never heard of these people and asked Paul who they were? He told Alan to listen to Radio Luxembourg, telling him, 'tune into medium wave 208 on Saturday and Sunday, 8pm until midnight'. Alan was curious as to what the music was that had made Paul so excited and sat in his own house

Alan with his athletics team mates and trophy. (Courtesy of Iris Caldwell)

waiting for 8.00 p.m. to arrive. It did, and the show began. The music played and Alan was stunned, for he had never heard anything like it. The music had him tapping his hands and feet. It was magical and he loved it. He wanted a guitar like Paul so he too could play this music. Then he heard Bill Haley, later Elvis Presley, and with them Rock 'n' Roll. He was mesmerised. This is what he wanted in his life. The music fitted his zany persona. A star was born.

Alan won the 3 miles Wood Cup in 1956, beating a field of over 100 runners. Once more he came with a late burst of speed to take the race easily. To the astonishment of the watching crowd, Alan was heard singing 'Rock around the clock' at the top of his voice. As he entered the final yards of the race he slowed to a walk, all so that he could cross the finish line as the song ended. This was becoming a kind of trademark for Alan in many of his races, and it was starting to upset many of the competitors who thought him big-headed. But Alan cared nothing for what they thought; his ego was everything. *The Daily Post* reported on the race, giving Alan a great review and mentioning his clear talent for running. They also noted that his time of 17 minutes dead would have been a lot faster if he had sprinted to the finish and not walked it while making his strange cries. Charles Gains of the Liverpool and Pembroke

Happy family: Ernie, Iris, Alan, and Vi. (Courtesy of Iris Caldwell)

Harriers Athletic Club has kindly allowed two articles from the club's 1950s magazine *Ace of Clubs* to be reproduced here.

3000 Metres Steeplechase
Club Championship
Port Sunlight, August 1958

Barry Juxon led right up to the water jump, but at the last moment he could not clear it. To everyone's amazement he climbed over the obstacle, with the rest of the field passing him. The runners began spreading out and Arthur Prescott was seen to be leading from Geoff Warriner and Eddie Williams. Alan Caldwell, with his reputation at stake, was lying 4th.

The leading positions remained the same until with two and a half laps to go Arthur started dropping back, and Eddie opened up a small lead on Geoff. Champion Caldwell, was lying handy ten yards behind. Things were now certainly warming up with Alan passing Geoff Warriner then challenging Eddie Williams. Alan took the lead at the water jump. From then on it was virtually all over. Caldwell, looking quite fresh, drew further and further away from the field to win the

The familiar sight of a well-clear Alan during a race. (Courtesy of Iris Caldwell)

first ever Club Steeplechase Championship from Eddie Williams, with Warriner finishing a very gallant, but tired, third.

Everybody finished the course and it was a grand success, even though Alan Caldwell presented the trophy to himself. Incidentally, the beggar has started training already for next year's race. Result, 1st Alan Caldwell-9 mins 38 secs, 2nd Eddie Williams-9 mins 50 secs. 3rd Geoff Warriner-9 mins 54 secs.

ACE OF CLUBS
Sept/Oct 1957

The initial dance to the Pembroke social season was held at the Broadway Hall on Saturday 19th October. It was voted a successful dance by many of those in attendance, and as well as being a financial success, it seems the social committee have made a good job of their dual role of entertainers and finance raisers.

No little part was played by the king of Skiffle – 'All Your Own' Alan Caldwell, who together with his group, put on some vivid entertainment for the assembled personnel. We look forward to having them at our next dance.

While brushing his teeth in the bathroom at the back of his house in Broad Green Road, Alan would often hear someone playing a guitar. He could not figure out where the sound was coming from, but it was

The scrapbook that Alan kept, inside of which he wrote details about his races. The book is very big and contains many clippings from newspapers, as well as photographs and race results. (Courtesy of Iris Caldwell)

a decent player that he could hear, who knew the Rock 'n' Roll songs from radio Luxembourg. If he could only find the guitar player, then who knows? They clearly shared the same interest in music, maybe they could do something together? But first, Alan needed a guitar.

2

Rave Me a Texan

In 1956, Alan was given a tip for a horse that was running in the Grand National. He went along to Aintree racecourse, where he placed a big bet on the horse 'Devon Loch' before looking for a viewing spot near the finish line. If the horse won he could afford the guitar he was so eager to obtain. As the race unfolded, it was clear for all to see that Devon Loch was moving really well. Over the last fence the horse zoomed clear, reaching the elbow of the run-in with an unassailable lead. Alan was counting his money. The horse then jumped into the air and bellyflopped onto the floor. It appeared that he had seen the wings of the water jump and tried to take off. ESB ran past to victory, leaving Alan mortified.

Alan was furious as he boarded the bus home and went upstairs for a seat. As he simmered his anger he heard a guitar playing. Looking up, he saw a young lad strumming away and went over to chat to him. His name was John Byrne and it turned out that he lived at No. 37 Oakhill Park, which was right behind Alan's house. After telling him about the horse and the guitar that he so nearly had, he felt a little better. John told Alan he could use his guitar. Alan could not play, but John said that he would teach him. As he watched John play his music on that bus, it dawned on him that this was the guitar player that he had heard from his bathroom window. Ernie was furious when he discovered that Alan had bet on the horse and warned him about the dangers of gambling. He did however give him the money to buy the guitar, feeling that Alan deserved it after all he had done to help out the family. An Egmond guitar was bought, and a firm friendship was formed between Alan and John as they played their guitars together, with John teaching Alan how to play the chords.

John was born on 4 December 1939 in Liverpool to Michael Patrick Byrne, a Seaman, born 22 October 1908, and Elsie Ford, who had married in the city in 1932. Elsie was born 10 July 1905 in Liverpool, with her early years being spent at No. 2 Belfast Road in Old Swan. Here she lived with her one sister and four brothers, her mother Eliza (nee Cowan) and her father Henry, who worked as a coal dealer. Her parents had married in 1898 and moved to the Old Swan area from Everton. By 1933 Michael and Elsie were living in London, where they had their first two children, Patrick and Norma. The family returned to Liverpool when Michael's work was moved there. After their return, John and Paul were born. John was a pupil at St Oswald's school in Old Swan and a part of the church of the same name. Like Alan, John had taken dance lessons at Martin's school on Derby lane. They had both attended the boys' club there as well. Just before his teen years John was struck down with rheumatic fever. He pulled through and spent six months in a Southport hospital convalescing.

Alan attended an athletics event in London, taking the train from Lime Street along with many other competitors. He had taken his guitar with him, and on the journey home a lad named Norman Wilson recognised Alan as the singing runner. He liked his guitar and asked could he play it. Norman was very good on it, playing many of the popular chart songs, but it was Alan who stole the show. Jumping up he started to sing along to Norman's playing, leaping on seats and running down the train aisles. Everyone clapped and sang along with him. Alan was given a good feeling from this; he had found his forte.

After seeing Lonnie Donegan in concert, John and Alan were both on a high and decided to form a band. They talked into the night about how fame would come to them, and of all the big theatres that they would play in. Vi had woken and could hear them chatting from her bed. Often she giggled to herself at their excitement, but most of all she felt pride,

Alan pictured while running a road race. (Courtesy of Iris Caldwell)

for Alan as he was happy with what he was doing. Reg Hales joined them on washboard, John Carter on guitar, and Jim Turner playing the Tea-chest bass. 'Alan Caldwell's Skiffle Group' was born. They had thought about having the name 'Dracula and the Werewolves' but decided against it – probably for the best really. The Werewolves was an odd choice of name as John was terrified of them. He loved horror films and collected the comics, but werewolves really scared him, so much so that he was afraid to walk home from Alan's house when it was a full moon, even though he could have run there in around 20 seconds. Alan, Iris and Vi would tell him not to be silly and convinced him to walk home. Ernie would then run around and hide on John's wall until he appeared, before jumping out to scare him. No wonder he was worried.

Faron Ruffley (later of Faron and The Flamingos) had become friends with Alan and John through their mutual interest in music. Faron was playing with a skiffle band named The Odd Spots, as well as attending university and working for a law firm in Water Street. The firm had a strong-room in the basement with a steel door. The files of large clients were kept inside, along with anything valuable. Faron's only interest in

Alan with another trophy to add to his collection. (Courtesy of Iris Caldwell)

the room was using it as somewhere to practice his music. John would come around from his job at the Cotton Exchange and jam with Faron. Others did as well, including a number of female admirers. One day, as they were all singing away, they heard a loud knock on the door. Faron told everyone to hide and began to climb the steps to the steel door. As he did, he feared that this could be the end of his career with the law firm. Faron opened the door and all he could see was a tall dark figure standing there. The light behind it was shining around the body of the figure, giving it an angelic appearance. Then the figure spoke: 'c-can I c-come in as w-well'. Alan had arrived, and became part of the sessions that took place there almost every working day.

Al Caldwell's skiffle band found a number of local gigs around the Old Swan area, at places such as St Brendan's Hall, The Old Swan Pub (Known as The White House) The Black Horse Pub, St Oswald's church hall, St Paul's church hall, Brockman Hall at St John's church in Tue Brook, and on Derby Lane at Old Swan youth club and Martin's dance centre. They went down pretty well and were getting themselves noticed. Alan had become the lead singer; his stutter disappeared when he sang. Many people have commented that they were shocked that Alan did not stutter during singing, but it is well known through medical practice that you cannot stutter while singing unless you mean to do it. The author of this book had a terrible stammer as a child and was taught to speak clearly by singing the words. Alan had sung at the football matches and with his father, but this was a different matter. He both feared and craved it, with John telling him he must sing as he was so good at it, and that he was born to be a frontman.

A glimpse of the risks that Alan and John were prepared to take for music were seen on 20 February 1957 at the Liverpool Odeon cinema, when the two friends wanted to see Bill Haley and The Comets perform. Alan had bought a ticket but John had missed out, and as the tickets had all been sold, a plan was hatched to get him into the concert. From his house Alan took two of Ernie's old work jackets from when he was at the Automatic Telephone & Electric Co. They both put them on and presented themselves at the side door of the Odeon on London Road. John told Alan to let him do the talking and informed the guy at the door that they were there to check the electrics. It worked, and he let them in; they went straight upstairs to look for a place to hide. A door led them to the projection room, where it was dark and perfect for hiding. They pushed a cupboard aside and hid behind it. Hour after hour crept past. The lads were nervous about being caught, but also found it all very funny. They heard music. It was the band doing their soundcheck. Time went by painfully slowly until at last they heard the noise of the public starting to enter. When Bill Haley was announced they seized their chance, removed the jackets, and mingled with the crowd who were heading up to the balcony. They made it through undetected and got to enjoy the concert. It blew them away and John could not take his eyes off the electric guitars; he could not stop thinking 'I must save. I must get myself one.'

Dave Jamieson, known to all as 'Jamo', met Alan on the kop during a Liverpool FC match in February 1957. Jamo had gone along with a few friends, and while there he had noticed a tall lad a little older than him standing by his friends. The lad never said a word until Liverpool scored. Then he tried to shout 'goal' and Jamo noticed how it took him so long to get the word out. Jamo stood next to Alan and told him 'I will shout goal for you'. The start of a lasting friendship was formed, and as they chatted after the game Alan found out that Jamo lived in Walton and attended the cadets on Edge Lane Drive, he told him to call at his house on Broad Green Road the following Monday after his cadets. Monday 25 February 1957 was Jamo's birthday and he kept his promise to call at Alan's house. Alan's mum Vi answered the door and informed him that he was out. She then said 'I suppose you are Jamo? Many happy returns, come on in'. Jamo went inside and saw another young lad playing a guitar. 'It is my birthday as well' said George Harrison.

A few weeks later Jamo was walking along St Oswalds Street in Old Swan with his cadet snare drum when he bumped into John and Alan, who were carrying guitars. John looked at the drum and said to Jamo, 'I suppose you are a drummer?' Jamo answered back, 'I suppose you are a guitarist?' Alan said, with a stammer, 'No, but we will be.' They explained they had formed a skiffle group and asked Jamo if he wanted to practice with them. He agreed and helped them out a few times. They would practice in the shed at the side of Alan's house, where Jamo would stand the snare drum on bricks and whack away as Alan and John sang 'Rock Island Line'. Jamo's cadet commitments kept him from joining the group, but they remained friends and he would often meet Alan in the record shop on Breck Road in Anfield.

On 24 May 1957, the band descended the steps of a warehouse cellar in Matthew Street having been booked to play at a jazz club called 'The Cavern'. The show included The Muskrat Jazz Band and The Gin Mill Skiffle Group, and was no great earth-shaker. However, its importance in musical history cannot be overlooked, as they became the first band to set the roots of what was to become the centre of the Liverpool Beat scene. It was believed to have been enhanced further, nineteen days later on 12 June, when The Quarrymen and their lead singer John Lennon are thought to have joined Alan Caldwell's Skiffle Group for a session at The Cavern.

The band was now focused on getting gigs anywhere. Experience was needed, so they agreed to almost everything. Community centres, Boys clubs, friends' parties, weddings, coffee shops, if there was room then they would play. Alan was a natural frontman, dancing around and singing, and generally making the band noticeable. Even the social club at the exotic-sounding 'Stanley Abattoir' bore witness to the talents of the boys who entertained the paying public there. Alan started dating a girl named Jean Baxter, a first for him to stay with a girl longer than a week as his shyness and stutter tended to put him off relationships. Jean would go along to the bands gigs to support Alan. He was great on stage, but could get nervous before a performance. Jean would often give him a kiss and a hug to reassure him, and on the odd occasion a shove to get him up there.

On 22 June, John and Paul Murphy from Heliers Road went along to the Percy Phillips recording studio in Kensington. They asked to make a record and were shown into the studio. The studio was more of a room with heavy curtains covering the windows and doors in an attempt to keep out the street noise. Recordings were made on tape before being transferred to disc. Often it would require a few takes if a bus or lorry rushed past and was caught on the playback. John and Paul recorded Little Richard's 'She's Got It', along with a popular song called 'Butterfly'. The recordings were transferred to a disc and are believed to be the first made by anyone associated with the Merseybeat era. Billy Fury, Ken Dodd, The Quarrymen and many others also record at the studio before hitting the big time.

In addition to impressing friends with his disc, John could play it to charm the ladies, who he liked very much. Another one of his techniques was to invite a girl along to the Curzon cinema in Old Swan. Here, he would buy two tickets for the horror film that he had checked earlier was being shown. His hope must have been that the girl would become frightened during the film and fall into his arms. He was just a young lad really, trying to have some fun. Sadly, as this book was being written, the wonderful building that was the Curzon cinema was bulldozed to the ground. John would have been mortified. One of John's early relationships was with a girl named Pat Hesketh from Danescourt Road in West Derby. It was an often rocky affair as emotions and the innocence of youth took hold.

Iris came home with her first boyfriend when she was twelve – a lad from Speke called George Harrison. They would hold hands while watching TV, or go for walks and kiss and cuddle. It was all very innocent and sweet. George had noticed how her brother Alan was always running and checking his times on a stopwatch. He also noticed that he played in a band, and as George himself was a decent guitar player he became interested in them. He made it known to Alan that he would like to join his band, but he was too young for them, and they and Vi had to turn him down. Alan also told him that he could not move and play so he was no good to them. He did try to teach George a few steps, but he was hopeless.

The Curzon Cinema in Old Swan, chatting-up ground of John Byrne. Iris Caldwell danced here as a child during film intervals. Sadly this fine building was demolished during the writing of this book.

Alan knew a Mrs Thompson who lived in a large Victorian house called Balgownie, at No. 25 Oakhill Park, very close to John's house and around the corner from Alan's. They were allowed to practice in her rather dark basement, thus keeping Alan's neighbours happily out of earshot from the noise. The band kept searching for gigs to play, and were allowed back at The Cavern on 3 January 1958, followed by another session there five days later. They also now gave themselves a name change, becoming 'Al Caldwell's Texans'.

A few weeks later they submitted an entry for the Jim Dale Skiffle contest that was being held at the Empire theatre. They were accepted and made it through the heats on 5 March, before getting through to the semi-finals the following night. On the 7 March they appeared in the final, losing to a group called Darktown. It had been a fantastic effort and valuable experience for the band, playing in front of such a large crowd in a big arena. The Texans also took part in a competition at the Locarno Ballroom on West Derby Road. They were placed third and Alan went mad. He started calling the judges every name under the sun and demanded that they did a recount of the votes. He told them 'no way have

Alan and John performing at a party. (Courtesy of Iris Caldwell)

we come third'. The votes were counted again and it was discovered that the result was wrong. The Texans had been placed third by mistake when they actually had finished fifth.

Alan and John came up with the idea of turning the cellar at Balgownie into a club where bands could play. After clearing it with Mrs Thompson they set to work with a number of art students, painting the walls black before adding skeletons onto them. A strip light was also added, posters made and a name chosen – 'The Morgue'. The club opened on 13 March 1958, without permission from the authorities of course. With no licence they could not charge an entry fee, but did insist that those entering bought a soft drink, though no toilets were available. The opening night was a success, with The Texans playing alongside The Quarrymen, who featured a John Lennon and a Paul McCartney. That same week they played a student dance at the art college in Hope Street and a school dance at Childwall Valley girls' school.

The Morgue was open on a Tuesday and Thursday. Around it they played at The Cavern and The La Boheme in Wallasey. One night at The Morgue attracted over 100 people – a remarkable turnout and proof of the club's popularity. The Bluegenes, who would later become The Swinging Blue Jeans, played there on one occasion. The Morgue however had an enemy in the shape of Mr Brown who lived next door. He was not happy about the noise, bottles in gardens, or the smooching couples who he saw through his window. Mr Brown got in touch with the authorities, who sent the police round for a visit on 1 April. Alan did his best to reassure them that he would do all that he possibly could to keep the revellers under control, and he did, making and erecting posters asking people to be as quiet as possible on leaving, signing them 'Alan Caldwell, Manager'. However, Mr Brown was on a mission, and his constant complaints forced the club's closure on 22 April 1958. The following day he turned up at Mrs Thompson's house with other angry residents, demanding that The Morgue stay closed. Mrs Thompson had no option but to agree, and just six weeks after it opened The Morgue was no more.

The importance of The Morgue must never be underestimated in terms of musical history. It not only proved the need for a venue to host up-and-coming bands, but it played a big part in what was to come. George Harrison auditioned for The Quarrymen here, leading to his teaming up with John and Paul. Sadly, Balgownie no longer stands, having fallen victim to the bulldozer. St Agnes School was built on the site, but that also fell to demolition; housing now stands in its place.

Alan's sister Iris had pestered him about allowing her to go to The Morgue. She had just turned fourteen and was too young to go, but like her brother was a rather determined character. Iris stuffed cotton wool into her bra in an attempt to make herself look older, and off she went to the club. Later that evening Alan got up on the stage and announced to everyone that his little sister was in the crowd with a bra stuffed with cotton wool. Iris was so ashamed she ran outside in tears, followed by George Harrison, who caught her up, gave her a kiss, and told her everything was fine. She and George became and stayed an item in their sweet way until he attended a party at her house. While playing a game the boys were ushered into the kitchen, while the girls were all given a fruit name. When the boys returned they were asked by Iris's mother Violet what fruit they wanted, before being sent over to a girl with that fruit name to give her a kiss. When asked, George was directed to a friend of Iris who he did not like, before announcing 'I am not hungry'. Iris was so angry at the insult to her friend that she asked George to leave and never to speak to her again.

Alan had gone to London on 11 April for a cross-country event. After the race he visited the Two I's bar and Chas McDevitt's Skiffle cellar in the hope of attracting the attention of one of the music promoters, jumping up on stage to sing with the playing band at McDevitt's, giving his all, and attracting the attention of a radio Luxembourg producer. This led to the Texans recording a version of 'Midnight Special' in Manchester, which was broadcast on Radio Luxembourg's Skiffle programme on 30 April. Jim Turner left the band after the closure of The Morgue, being replaced on bass by Jeff Trueman. He played at The Cavern and Liverpool

University with The Texans, before deciding it was not for him. Spud Ward then took over on bass duties.

On 7 June Alan and John jumped aboard the late Crosville bus to Pwllheli in Wales. Their destination, Butlins, and 'The People's National Talent Competition'. The next day they sailed through the auditions to huge cheers. It was noticeable that the other two group members were not with them. With just four days to go to the final they managed to recruit a bass and washboard player. In the final they played 'Rock Island Line' and 'John Henry' and the crowd loved them. They were crowned the winners, with a prize of £3 and a free holiday. Playing in a large theatre to a cheering crowd had once more boosted their ego, and they returned to Liverpool feeling like stars. They also had a fine time chasing the ladies, but agreed not to chat up any Liverpool girls in case they had an angry boyfriend back home.

That summer brought shows at the Cavern, Liverpool University, Winter Gardens talent contest in Garston, and over the river in Wallasey. On 17 July they played at the Liverpool show held in the Mystery Park, Wavertree. In September, Paul Murphy from Heliers Street joined the band; he played guitar and sang. On 25 July Alan threw Spud Ward out of the band, although he was soon back playing with them. Alan appeared at one gig with a huge boil on his face. He produced a paper bag with holes cut out for the eyes and mouth, before slotting it over his head. The boil was now gone and he played the whole show wearing the bag. John started a job with the post office on 19 December, and although

Alan and John at Butlins where they won the talent contest. (Courtesy of Iris Caldwell)

he never remained there long, it appears to be one of the few jobs that he actually enjoyed doing. The year 1958 tailed off with not many gigs for them, though they remained upbeat and ready for a new year.

John and Alan with guitars, posing at The People's National Talent Competition in Butlins, Pwllheli. (Courtesy of Iris Caldwell)

On 6 January 1959 Alan quit his job at the Cotton Exchange, telling his parents that he wanted to play music full-time. Ernie was in despair, but Vi was delighted. The next day Alan turned twenty-one. Vi now became the manager of the band, taking bookings through Winnie Mac's phone (STO 3324) over the road from her house. She also had cards printed that read 'Downbeat Productions', which she handed out at possible venues. In February they managed to get a booking at the Madri Gras on Mount Pleasant, where once again they were told to play Jazz or Skiffle. They decided to look for a place that would host Rock 'n' Roll, even asking people with large buildings if they could rent out their cellar. They thought that they had found a place at the church house of St Paul's on Derby Lane, the house standing opposite the church at the side of Derwent Road. The church was willing to allow them use of the cellar, but the plans fell through, leaving the lads without a venue. When would the world move on from jazz?

Roy Rich joined the band in February 1959, though nobody can recall what he actually did. Gigs followed at Liverpool University, Kraal Jazz club in New Brighton, Alexandra Hall, Crosby, The Cavern and a club called The Catacombs. The *Liverpool Echo* listed them in a Cavern advert as 'Al Caldwell and his Jazzmen' on 26 February, something that they would not have been happy about. On 25 March they played at the Madri Gras, with Richard Starkey filling in on drums. In the audience watching was a certain Walter Eymond. By the start of April Paul Murphy and Roy Rich had left the band, with Charles O'Brien coming in on lead guitar and vocals after an audition at Alan's house. A new era was beginning to take shape for the band.

Charles was born Charles William O'Brien in Liverpool on 15 February 1941, to Charles William O'Brien, born 1906 in Liverpool, and Marie Brierly, born 2 October 1904 in Liverpool. The couple married in 1927 at St Michael and Sacred Heart church on West Derby Road, Liverpool. The family lived at No. 49 Pemberton Road, Old Swan, with Charles Snr working as a seaman for the Canadian Pacific Line. Charles had an older sister named Marie who had been born in 1928. She loved him so and doted after him. In 1911, Charles's grandparents, Francis Brierly, a merchant seaman born in Roscrea in County Tipperary, Ireland, and Mary Stewart, born Liverpool, were living at No. 68 Argos Road in Kirkdale, Liverpool, having married in 1896. His other grandparents, Edward John O'Brien, a biscuit baker by trade, and Ada Alice Wright, had both been born in Liverpool and were married in the city in 1899. In 1911, Edward and Ada were living at No. 21 Greenside, behind the collegiate school on Shaw Street.

Young Charles became a very talented amateur boxer, training at the Derby Lane gym, as well as a very good guitar player. He had been a pupil at St Oswald's school, and attended the church there. Charles, or Chas as he was often called, had known John Lennon and The Quarrymen in their early days. He was also another member of the band who had attended Martin's dance school on Derby Lane in Old Swan, where he proved to be a rather decent dancer. To reach the dance centre he basically had to walk out of his front door and take a left, before walking across Derby lane – a 2-minute walk. Charles was talented enough to become part of a dance formation team. He was also a great limbo dancer, amazingly being able to get under a bar just 12 inches off the ground. He had found himself a decent job as a joiner's apprentice and was very skilled at the craft. He explained to the band that he would be working there on weekdays. Charles first played with the group on 4 April 1959, at the Alexandra Hall in Crosby. It was no great earth-shattering event; in fact it was a pretty awful performance. They then cancelled a number of gigs because the money offered was too low.

John Byrne took at job with a company called Platt's at the Cotton Exchange, though he hated it and never stayed long. They wrote to the TV shows *Oh Boy!* and *Drumbeat* in hope of auditions. The BBC wrote back explaining that *Drumbeat* was not holding any auditions, while ITV responded with 'Please write again at the end of August'. On 7 May they played at the Hope Cinema in Hope Street (now The Everyman Theatre), outside of which they tasted stardom when they were mobbed by a group

St Oswald's Church, Old Swan. The old school building can be seen towards the left, taken from the school playing field. John and Charles attended the church and school here as children.

of girls hunting autographs. Gigs followed at the St Agnes Labour Club in Huyton and the Dyson Memorial Hall in Kensington, before playing at The Cavern on 21 May. The following day they found themselves a drummer in the shape of Richard Starkey. A quick practice session was arranged before they did a two-night stint at The Cavern between 23–24 May.

Richard had been born on 7 July 1940, at No. 9 Madryn Street in the Dingle area of Liverpool, to Richard Starkey and Elsie Gleave, who had married in 1936. The couple had spent time dancing together on the ballroom circuit, but the birth of Richard drove them apart. Richard Snr showed little interest towards his son, preferring to spend his time drinking in local pubs. Elsie raised Richard and doted after him. In 1944 they moved the short distance to No. 10 Admiral Grove, the move being done by loading their possessions onto a handcart. Within a year Richard Snr had left and a divorce had been completed; his son barely saw him again.

Richard, known as Ritchie, was very ill as a child, developing appendicitis aged six that led to a stay in the Myrtle Street children's hospital. He was a pupil at St Silas primary school and Dingle Vale secondary school, where he was a classmate of Billy Fury. In 1953 he contracted tuberculosis and was admitted to the children's hospital at Heswell on the Wirral. Elsie married a Londoner called Harry Graves in the same year, a kind man who Ritchie liked and looked up to. Harry encouraged Ritchie to follow his dreams. So much illness had caused him problems at school and he played truant a lot, before leaving to find work. After a few failed attempts, it was his step-father Harry who found him an apprenticeship making climbing frames.

Ritchie had a huge interest in music, and it took off when he joined his co-workers Roy Trafford and Eddie Miles to form The Eddie Miles Band, later changing the name to Eddie Clayton and The Clayton Squares. At first Ritchie hit a wooden or tin box for a drum, or scratched a tune from a washboard. His step-father Harry presented him with a battered and basic second-hand drum kit on Christmas Day 1957, and Ritchie was over the moon. The band sounded better and gained a number of gigs.

Ritchie played a few more times with The Texans, including a couple of gigs at The Cavern, before the Dyson Memorial Hall gig on 15 June 1959 which saw the departure of Reg Hales and Spud Ward. The band had by now renamed themselves 'Al Caldwell and his Raving Texans'. Ritchie used the phone at Jones newsagents near his house as a contact number. Another Old Swan lad, Walter Eymond, was brought in on bass. John bought his Antoria guitar from a man in Prescot Street on 29 June for £29 – a tidy sum back then. For their first gig together the band played at the University of Liverpool on 1 July. Nothing of great interest to report about the occasion – again not a great performance – but these five lads were now together, the classic five that people remember them as, and many things were about to change.

Walter Eymond was born Walter Lewis Eymond on 6 August 1938 off Cazneau Street in Liverpool. His parents, who had married in Liverpool in 1934, were Henry Lewis Eymond, born 1906, and Mary Melia. Henry was the son of Lewis Felix Eymond and Georgina Esther Carruthers (Walter's grandparents) who in 1911 were living at No. 13 Buckingham Road in Walton, Liverpool, with Lewis working as a ship's pattern-maker. Walter's great-grandfather, Jean-Marie Henri Eymond, had brought his family over to England from the Bordeaux region of France. In 1875 he was living in the Dingle area of Liverpool and working as a master mariner. Walter also had a sister named Jean who had been born in 1935. During the Second World War Walter's home was bombed, resulting in the family being rehoused at No. 11 Ulster Road in Old Swan for the remainder of the war. Walter's father Henry worked as an electrical engineer and would often take his family with him when he worked in such places as London, Newcastle and Dudley in Birmingham.

If you look up Walter's birth record it states that he was born in Prescot. This is untrue as he was born off Cazneau Street, just outside Liverpool city centre. When his home had been bombed during the Second World War, his birth certificate was destroyed. When he needed a new one he was sent to Prescot to register, and they marked down that he was born there. That however, is a mistake.

By the early 1950s the family had settled at No. 20B The Green. This was one of the flats in the blocks behind the Gardeners Arms public house and was very close to Alan and John's houses. Aged around eight, Walter's singing abilities were recognised when he became part of the choir at St Paul's church on Derby Lane in Old Swan. Walter had attended the same school as Alan at Highfield, which was right behind the block where he lived. He was in the year below him, but knew him to talk to. Walter recalled, 'Alan was a very good Athlete who I would watch when I was training for my own athletics events such as the discus. Alan was also known for sitting at the back of classes singing Johnnie Ray songs before angry teachers would throw him out of the room.' Like Alan, John and Charles, Walter was a member of the Billy Martin's dance centre.

Walter and Charles O'Brien were already good friends by the time they joined The Hurricanes. Charles attended the Catholic school of St Oswalds, while Walter was at the C of E Highfield School. Of course back then the religious divide was still a small problem and the kids would hang around in their school gangs. One night both lads were at Billy Martin's dance centre on Derby Lane in Old Swan with their gang/schoolmates. When Walter went outside one of the Catholic lads told him he had to fight with one of his gang. Walter told him to 'get stuffed', before Charles came over and told them to lay off him. Walter laughed it off and said 'you're all nuts, I'm getting off', to which Charles replied 'I'm coming with you.'

Their friendship was formed and they found that they both had an interest in music. Charles could play the guitar, so with Walter on Tea Chest bass they formed a skiffle group called The Hi Fis. Charles's cousin Tommy also joined the band. They played a few gigs and entered a talent contest at the Carlton Cinema in Tue Brook, where they were joined by The Dusty Road Ramblers. Walter started work as an apprentice engineer with the Liverpool-based London company George Taylor (engineers), but like Charles, music was his love.

The first change to the band was their name – Al Storm and The Hurricanes. It was time to get serious, but not before Alan and John had returned from a short break at Butlins, Pwllheli. They really appeared to like it there. While at Butlins they watched Rory Blackwell and the Blackjacks, the band who had starred in the 1957 film *Rock You Sinners*. Rory sacked his guitarist and asked John to join them. He played a couple of times with them before he turned them down, and just for good measure Alan pinched his name and began playing around with words to fit around Rory. On the final day of their holiday, Alan won a swimming

Walter playing tea chest bass with his first band at Butlins in 1957. His friend Eddie, who also lived on The Green, is playing wash board, while another pal, Georgie, is strumming a guitar that belonged to Walter. The guy in the middle was from Northwich and is playing a bin. They won the talent contest and a large prize of £25. (Courtesy of Walter Eymond)

contest and received his prize standing in just his skimpy swimming trunks. A number of the ladies in the crowd made comments about his athletic physique, while one man shouted out 'you queer'. Alan replied back 'That's not what your wife said last night mate.' This caused the man to go for Alan, and he and John jumped from the stage and ran back to the chalet, picked up their things, and got themselves out of Butlins.

Alan striking a pose at Butlins. (Courtesy of Iris Caldwell)

The lads would practice in Alan's house. Ritchie would set his drums up in the hallway with the rest of the lads sitting on the stairs with guitars. They also rehearsed in Walter's house on The Green, where the downstairs neighbours had their nerves put to the test by the noise from up above. If it was a nice day then someone's garden would do as they tried out their set. Charles would also pop in to play the card game Gin Rummy with Vi and Iris, with Iris holding a secret crush for Charlie, as she called him.

The lads planned their rise to fame. They smartened the band up with jackets from C&A, new trousers and shoes. Bookings were being taken more regularly by this time, with John using a neighbour's telephone and Alan using the one at Winnie Mac's house for contact as neither had a phone in their own home. The lads practiced step routines for the band to perform behind Alan. Soon they would upgrade to 'made-to-measure' suits that cost them £50 each – a lot of money for the time, but it shows just how serious they were taking it all.

Perhaps the most important event during this period was that of Monday 10 August when they went to visit a Mrs Woods. The story goes that her son had bought himself a Framus 4 string electric bass guitar from Hessey's music shop, but she was having none of it as she thought it was far too expensive. Walter Eymond however thinks that the bass belonged to Mrs Woods' daughter who had gone away to work on the cruise ships. Hearing that she wanted to sell it, the lads called at her home, and after a bit of haggling they paid her £5 and agreed to sign the takeover of the hire purchase agreement. They were now all playing electric guitars, a real Rock 'n' Roll band. Three Semler amps were purchased, and Walter got to work practising with the new bass. At first they faced a few hitches: broken bass strings, trying to find new ones to buy, even attempting to solder the broken strings together, these guys would do anything. It all came together in the end, and they prepared to unleash it onto the public.

When Walter walked into St Luke's Hall in Crosby he was surrounded by members from other bands, all eager to take a look at the Framus bass. They took to the stage, burst into 'Brand New Cadillac' and blew everyone away. The deep boom of the bass thumped away, the guitars rang their tunes, the drums banged in time, and the crazy singer leapt around the stage. This was Rock 'n' Roll, and Liverpool had seen nothing like it before from a local band. The crowd loved it, as did the other bands. The local music shops were invaded over the coming weeks by young lads looking to buy electric bass guitars. Once again the band had become trendsetters, this time in a way that would change the Merseyside music scene forever.

Their fan base was growing and the bookings flew in. They were by now regulars at The Cavern and St Luke's Hall (The Jive Hive). The Locarno Ballroom on West Derby road booked them, as did The Lathom

Hall in Seaforth. They also played at Lowlands in Hayman's Green, West Derby, close to the home of Pete Best, who would later become The Beatles' drummer. Mona Best, mother of Pete, had opened a club in her cellar named The Casbah. The Hurricanes played there a few times, but the club already had a regular band in the shape of The Quarrymen.

They played a variety show in Rhyl on 23 August that was topped by the singer Marion Ryan, who had had a hit with the song 'Love Me Forever'. They closed the first set to a tremendous reception. This was a great experience for them; they were being noticed and getting bigger bookings. The £25 fee they received was also a step in the right direction. The ITV show *Oh Boy!* contacted them asking for photographs of the group, and they came second in the Carroll Levis Show at the Liverpool Empire. 150 acts had entered the contest, so it was a great achievement by them.

In November they renamed themselves 'Jett Storm and The Hurricanes'. They also adopted stage names. Alan became 'Rory Storm' using the name he had pinched from Rory Blackwell in Butlins. Their love of westerns shone through as John became 'Johnny Guitar', the name being taken from the 1954 movie with that name. Charles was christened 'Ty Brien' after Ty Hardin of the TV show *Bronco*. Ritchie was given the name 'Ringo Starr'. First it was 'Rings', as he wore so many rings on his fingers, but Ringo sounded better and more western. Starr was a shortening of Starkey. Walter became 'Lou Walters'. He was not named after a western character; they just thought this sounded good as a stage name. Alan and John were well up for the name changes, now insisting on being called Rory and Johnny. The other three were not as keen, and it took a while for them to adopt them.

The group was now getting fully booked, playing six or seven nights a week, often playing at one venue before rushing off to another. They had relied on bus travel to get them and their instruments around the city to gigs, but this was now impossible with the heavy amplifiers. Vans had to be hired and drivers sought, with Johnny's brother Pat often acting as roadie and taking all five of them in his Ford car while securing all the gear to the roof. The lads, apart from Walter Eymond, all applied for a driving licence so that they could share the driving duties. Walter already had his and had purchased a Thames Grey van. Dave 'Jamo' Jamieson had been helping the band get to and from gigs as he had the use of his father's Bedford Prefect car. By late 1959 he had borrowed a van from Joe Flannery and was helping the band move their amplifiers around. Jamo also sat in with the lads as they practiced their driving skills with L-plates on a car. They were busy and much sought after, drawing a crowd wherever they played, so club owners wanted them, and they rocked, and rocked good.

Walter playing guitar in the living room of his home at No. 20B The Green. (Courtesy of Walter Eymond)

A new decade was approaching, and with it a change in music history. Merseyside was a hotbed of musical talent that was just waiting to explode into the 1960s. On top of its tree sat Rory, Johnny, Ty, Lou and Ringo, under their newly adopted name of 'Rory Storm and The Hurricanes'.

3

The Hurricanes Roar

The year 1960 started as it had ended for Rory Storm and The Hurricanes – busy! busy! busy! – not that they were complaining, with money in their pockets and plenty of female attention. New Year's Day saw them taking the train to Southport for a gig at the Cambridge Hall. A huge fight broke out as they played – something they would witness many more times in the future. The following day they were off to play in Ormskirk. They got there by taking a bus (around 13 miles). Do van drivers not work over New Year? Such is the life of a rock star, buses and trains. Johnny met a girl named Eileen Manson on 9 January 1960, who lived at No. 29 Brewery Lane in Freshfield, Formby. They got off to a rocky start, but they were smitten with each other and were soon going steady.

The Hurricanes' main problem was that they were a Rock 'n' Roll band and a lot of the clubs still wanted them to stick to the Skiffle numbers. In January 1960, The Cavern owner Ray McFall put on a Jazz festival at the club. It started on 10 January, with The Hurricanes being booked to play alongside The Bluegenes and The Mickey Ashman band on the 17 January. They were again informed to stick to playing Skiffle, but the temptation became too much and they burst into what is claimed to be either 'Brand New Cadillac' or 'Whole Lotta Shakin Goin On'. Whatever song it was the punters did not like it and made their feelings known by throwing coins at the band. Ray McFall was furious and halved their pay. While Rory argued with him, Johnny picked up all the coins from the stage, and after counting them they were better off than their original fee. If only the punters and Ray had known how important Rock 'n' Roll was to become to this club in just a short time ...

The following week they played at The Cavern again. DJ Bob Wooler introduced the band and their set was recorded – Vi Caldwell later taped a Cliff Richard radio show over it. Ray McFall had made a loss with his Jazz festival, and as a businessman he soon realised that Rock 'n' Roll was now the most popular music in the city. It was not long before he would be inviting The Hurricanes and similar bands to play at the club. His decision to do this would turn The Cavern into the most famous music club in the world, producing one of the biggest bands ever seen.

The Jive Hive (St Luke's Hall) The Cavern, The Casbah, Cambridge Hall in Southport, and Holyoake Hall on Smithdown Road all became regular venues for The Hurricanes during the first half of 1960. They would slot in other bookings as and when they could, such as St George's Hall, The Jacaranda, Grosvenor Hall in Wallasey, Lowlands in West Derby, Carr Mill in St Helens, The Casino in Southport, and The Corinthian in Seel Street. They were playing almost every night now, as well as holding down day jobs. Rory was also still competing at athletics, so was in training a lot. Often he would decide to run home after concerts to keep up his fitness, which shows the kind of dedication the members had for their band. Rory had even donated a trophy to his athletic club, The Pembroke Harriers. It was called the Rory Storm Trophy and was awarded to the winner of the 3000-metre steeplechase. Rory won the trophy himself twice. The trophy is now held at Liverpool museum, though it is not on display.

The Hurricanes were by now one of the top bands in Liverpool. Their thumping sound and stage gimmicks brought them plenty of attention. Rory was not the greatest singer in the world, and there were better musicians on the scene than the lads in the band. But they fitted and had a great stage presence; teamed with Rory's personality it made them an exciting group to watch. Rory was a law unto himself, unpredictable and mesmerising. He would leap from the stage, jump onto pianos, climb stage curtains, or kick his leg over a band mate's shoulder and dance across the stage. You just never knew what he was going to do next. When Lou took the vocal for songs such as 'Fever' or 'Beautiful Dreamer', Rory would take out a huge oversized comb and run it through his wild blonde hair while making sure to smile at the girls. As a frontman he was pure genius; nobody had seen anything like him in Liverpool. People flocked to watch this rocking band with its crazy singer. Rory was known as 'The King of Liverpool' and he loved the title, as he did his home city. His mother Vi would tell his sister Iris, 'He may be the king of Liverpool, but you are the Queen of Broad Green.'

For the St George's Hall gig on 1 April 1960, Rory had gone along to the hall days before and sought out the local promoter Sam Leach. Sam had booked the band a number of times before, yet never really sat and chatted with them. Rory told him The Hurricanes would play and did his standard fee haggle before an agreement was reached. He then invited Sam to join him for a coffee over the road at the Punch and Judy cafe. Here, as the two guys talked, they found they had a common love for Liverpool football club. Then, Rory told Sam that he would have to pay

Iris Caldwell in costume pose. (Courtesy of Iris Caldwell)

for the drinks as he had left his money in his car, but he did offer to drive him to Barnsley the next day to see their team play. Sam accepted and a firm friendship was formed.

Rory's sister Iris had always wanted to work at Butlins and was excited when she attended an audition for a dancer in London. She performed her routine and attempted to finish with a high-kick, but as she kicked she slipped and slid underneath the table with her head sticking out. One of the ladies present leant over her and said 'it's alright dear, you have passed'. A delighted Iris jumped up and asked if her brother could play at Butlins with his band, and was told they would need to contact the agent Herbert De Vere. Iris ran out of the building and headed to Mr De Vere's office. As she did she saw an old man walking with two walking sticks and spun him round before shouting 'I am going to Butlins.' When she arrived at De Vere's office she was informed that he had gone along to the auditions, so she ran back there and sought him out, only to find he was the man she had spun around in the street earlier. Iris got the job, and with it a ten-hour contract as a Red Coat. She was so proud when she put on that iconic red jacket.

Rory, on the advice of his sister Iris, had written to Butlins asking them to consider the band for a summer season in Pwllheli. He explained that they were the resident band at The Cavern and The Jive Hive. He also added that Clinton Ford, ex-Butlin Red Coat and recording singer, would be happy to vouch for them. This letter resulted in an audition on 16 February at the Rialto Ballroom. The auditions were held in the day and a number of the bands taking part would be invited to perform at the 'Butlins Ball' that was taking place at the Rialto that same evening. The Hurricanes blew the Butlins board away and were basically and unofficially informed that they would be hired. Then, they were asked to play at that evening's Butlins Ball. Most bands would have agreed on the spot and played to impress the board. However, most bands never had Rory, who asked the board how much they would be getting to play. They explained that the bands play for free at the ball, to which Rory replied 'we don't do anything for nothing', and gestured to the lads that it was time to leave. The board members wanted them, called them back, and agreed a fee of £5 for their services. A week later they found out that they had passed and would be playing the summer season at Pwllheli. Rory and Johnny were ecstatic, Ty and Lou happy but a bit unsure, and Ringo was terrified as he had his apprenticeship. They were offered £100 a week, less £20 accommodation. It was a big amount of money in 1960. The Butlins contract was not until June; the band still had a lot of engagements to fill before then.

Johnny, now the flash local rock star, decided that his image required a car. He bought a Jaguar, with his mother warning him not to become big-headed. Two weeks later, while taking Eileen for a spin, he decided to stop for petrol at the little station on Broad Green Road. It was just a strip of land with a wooden hut in the middle, either side of which stood two petrol pumps. Johnny drove in and managed to plough straight into the hut. Thankfully nobody was in there at the time. He soon sold the car at a loss. Rory had bought himself a Hillman Husky, while Ty purchased a red Zephyr. Ringo bought a red-and-white Vanguard from Johnny Hutch. Dave 'Jamo' Jamieson recalled Rory's Hillman Husky, saying 'It had that many holes in the floor that you could polish the tramlines on Scotland Road with your feet.' Jamo was laughing at the car to Rory's sister Iris at her house when she said 'Me and me mam have fixed it with plates from the oven.' Jamo went to look, and sure enough they had.

The Hillman was also the cause of a not so glamorous story. Rory and Iris, along with Johnny and his brother, had been to a party somewhere along Queens Drive. As they drove home smoke started to emerge from the engine. Rory stopped the car and opened the bonnet. As he did a huge ball of smoke burst into the air. Rory started shouting 'Oh no! The engines on fire.' Then, and to the horror of Iris, he shouted 'quick! Piss on it', and with that he popped out his member and began to urinate onto the car's engine. The other two lads did the same, but still the smoke rose quickly. Then, all eyes turned to Iris and the lads grabbed her, held her over the engine and told her to 'piss! Quick'. She was having none of it and refused point blank. Then, the cause of the fire was spotted: an oily rag that Rory had left in the engine that was smoking away. It was removed and they went on their way.

On 5 March The Hurricanes played The Jive Hive in Crosby. Their performance was recorded, but it is uncertain who ordered or did the recording. It was one of many recordings of the band, but its importance will be seen later in this book. On 3 May Rory Storm and The Hurricanes joined Gerry and The Pacemakers and Cass and The Cassanovas to back Gene Vincent at the Liverpool Stadium. To be considered good enough to be able to play on the bill with such a star of Vincent's calibre spoke volumes of how well thought of these three Liverpool groups were. As The Hurricanes opened up Rory was nowhere to be seen. The other band members just kept playing the intro to 'Honey Don't' – on and on it went. People began to look at one another, all wondering what was going on. Then, and picking his moment to perfection, Rory appeared. Johnny Guitar introduced him: 'Here he is, the sensational Rory Storm.' Ever so slowly he moved towards the stage in the middle of the stadium, shaking hands and slapping high fives with the crowd before jumping up and bursting into song. The place erupted. They loved him. It was a huge risk by Rory, but he nailed it, proving his amazing talent as a showman. The fans, pumped up by Rory and The Hurricanes, were going crazy by the time Gene Vincent appeared. They rushed the stage in an attempt

Walter playing Johnny's guitar at The Cavern. (Courtesy of Walter Eymond)

to climb up; the situation was getting out of control. Then appeared Rory, standing at the front of the stage. He raised his arm to indicate to the crowd to move back. They followed his command and the show restarted. Without uttering a word, Rory had saved the day.

After gigs, the lads would often hang out in the Zodiac Coffee Club on Duke Street, along with other musicians. One night the guys came in with members from other bands and the owner sent them to the room upstairs. They were all sitting at a long table when they realised there were thirteen of them sitting there. It was suggested that they were all at 'The Last Supper', with Rory sitting at the head of the table as Jesus. A photograph was taken and later lent to a member of the press who never returned it. Sadly it appears it is now lost forever. Another time Rory was at the Zodiac waiting for a guy to return his car that he had lent him earlier in the day. The guy was hours late and Rory was starting to panic. He stood outside on Duke Street looking up and down the road for him. Finally, he spotted his car turning the corner and also saw it crash straight into a lamp post.

One potential problem they faced going to Butlins was if Lou would be called up to the army for national service. They had a guy named Frank as back up, but his mother refused to let him go. As it turned out though Lou was not called up and was free to go. Make no mistake the Butlins contract was a big thing for a group: decent and regular wages, plus exposure. It meant that they would have to turn professional and that this would be their way of making a living. Rory was happy as he had already packed in his job. Johnny was glad as he hated all the jobs he had taken anyway, while Lou and Ty both decided to do it and also gave up their jobs. Ty at first had to face his reluctant parents who wanted him to stay on and learn a trade. Ringo was the stumbling block as he was over halfway through his apprenticeship at Henry Hunts. Ringo was unsure if he wanted to chance leaving his job, plus he was also engaged to his girlfriend Geraldine, with plans to marry the following year. In the end the lads talked him round. Now they just needed to convince his parents who were dead against it – enter Rory. Ever convinced that he could do anything, Rory went along to see Ringo's parents. He had not reckoned with Elsie, who refused point blank to let Ringo leave his job. Rory resorted to getting on his knees, crying and begging them, but they still said no. As it was, Ringo decided to go anyway, breaking off his engagement to Geraldine. His parents were not very happy with Rory.

Billy Fury and his manager Larry Parnes came to the Wyvern club (now The Blue Angel) on Seel Street. They were looking for backing groups to use with either Billy himself or other singers in the Parnes stable. Parnes had been excited by the Liverpool bands he had seen the previous week at the boxing stadium show. Auditions had been organised at the club for 10 May. The Hurricanes did not take part as they had the Butlins booking, but they came along to watch. Rory always looked the part, immaculately dressed and groomed. He had his photo taken with Billy Fury, and looking at the picture it is hard to tell which one is the big star. Larry Parnes was wary of why Rory wanted the photograph, telling him not to use it for publicity. Rory just wanted his photo taken with Billy. The Beatles were at the audition and were booked to back Johnny Gentle on a tour of Scotland with Tommy Moore on drums. It is stated that nobody at the audition was given the offer to back Billy Fury; this is untrue. The Hurricanes may not have auditioned, but Parnes remembered them from the boxing stadium and asked them if they would back Billy, the condition being that they dump Rory. The lads gave an instant answer – no! Rory was their frontman so they would not be backing anyone else.

One thing that the Hurricanes faced was envy that could lead to threats and punch ups. When groups played the girls would dance, giving the lads in the clubs the opportunity to make their move, asking the girls for a dance and trying out their chat-up lines. When Rory and The Hurricanes played however, the girls would run to the front of the stage, often screaming in delight. Rory was 6 foot 2 inches, blonde, blue-eyed and handsome. He was also built like an athlete, and the girls went wild over him and the band. There was little chance for chatting up the girls when The Hurricanes were playing, and this angered a number of the lads at their gigs. Then, they had the boyfriends to contend with. One smile or a wink to a girl could result in an angry boyfriend fronting the group member. Trouble broke out in the crowd during one gig at the Aintree Institute. The Sparrow Hall gang was in the audience watching the show when a gang from Broadway came in. The fighting between them both soon started, and objects began to be flung in every direction. Rory was up on stage still singing during all this chaos, and had to dodge a number of chairs that had been aimed at him. But he carried on and finished the song amid all this mayhem.

During one performance in Southport a girl in the crowd was fixated with Ty, and he was giving her smiles back. Her boyfriend was in the club and made his feelings known to Ty, giving him threats of a beating. Ty had been a very good boxer, so it was not the cleverest idea to take him on. The guy decided he would do it with the help of his mates, telling Ty he would get him outside. The band told Ty they would back him up as they loaded their gear into the van, but he told them all to jump in and wait for him. He then faced the guy and knocked him flat out with one punch, before getting into the van himself. The friends of the guy knocked out began throwing stones at the van as it moved away. One smashed a window and hit Rory on the head; he was bleeding, but was OK – the joys of stardom. While on the subject of Southport, it is of interest to note that when playing there during the summer months both Rory and Ty

Rory Storm. (Courtesy of Iris Caldwell)

would go along in the daytime before a gig and earn a few bob working as life-savers on the beachfront.

Although they were a top group in Liverpool and about to turn professional, they were still young lads and acted accordingly. After a visit to the Casbah in West Derby, Rory and Johnny were waiting in the village for the number 61 bus back to Broad Green Road. Johnny noticed the ancient stocks that had once been used for petty criminals and decided to put himself in them. He was almost caught by a policeman during this attempt for laughs. After a business visit to Butlins in Pwllheli they drove back to Liverpool. On the way home they stopped at a stream, and Rory and Johnny pushed each other in the water. Rory was caught by a worker at Bootle railway station writing all over a wall. He was writing 'I Love Rory Storm' in big letters.

Rory's mother's friend Winnie Mac had asked the group to play for the old folks at the local railway club. They agreed, and Rory sang the Tommy Steele song 'I'm The Only Man on the Island' while Iris and her friend Anne danced in grass skirts. They then sang 'Que Sera Sera' with Rory singing 'When I was just a little boy, I asked my mother What will I be? Will I be handsome? Will I be rich? Here's what she said to me ... You Ain't nothing but a hound dog'. The amps went full blast to deafen them, and the shock of seeing Rory jump up onto a piano almost finished off a few of the old folk. The lads could often be found hanging out at 'The Pack of Cards', an old shop on Brownlow Hill that was waiting to be demolished to make way for the building of the Metropolitan Cathedral. Many of the local bands would hang out here, playing records or chatting. They also had the nerve and foresight to start their own fan club, selling membership to it to people at their gigs.

Rory being Rory had to do everything with style, car included. He once called at Johnny's house to tell him he had found a car, and told Johnny to come with him. Off they walked, through Old Swan, along Tue brook and up towards Anfield. Johnny kept asking 'how far is it?', with Rory replying 'nearly there'. But on they went, into the Everton district, with Johnny telling Rory 'I'm not a bloody athlete like you, where are we going?' Rory kept up the pace, with Johnny starting to lag at his side. Finally, they reached Scotland Road and arrived at a Robinson's Car Sales. Rory walked up to a shiny Vauxhall Cresta, beckoned over the salesman and told him that he would pay by cash. He then produced £800 from his inside coat pocket and handed it over. A tired Johnny went crazy: '£800 you had on you and you made us walk for fucking miles. You could have paid for the bus you tight bastard.' Rory cared nothing about Johnny's complaint; he had the flash car. Johnny had a blue Zodiac car, but it was so unreliable and was forever being pushed to the hill on Broad Green Road to try to get it started. A crossbow with loaded arrow sat as an ornament on the back shelf of the car, Johnny having picked

The Hurricanes at The Cavern. (Courtesy of Iris Caldwell)

it up on a trip abroad. Imagine that today: one look through your back window and you would be arrested for having a dangerous weapon.

Ray McFall asked Rory to play at the Cavern again. This time he wanted him to play Rock 'n' Roll. 'We don't come cheap', said Rory. 'We play everywhere now, we are in demand. You have to pay us £10 now, and we want the money back that you docked us from that gig in January.' Ray nodded and agreed. He had no choice; he needed them. The 25 March saw Ray McFall go all out with a Beat Night at the Cavern. Cass and The Casanovas joined The Hurricanes in making music history by hitting the first notes of the Merseybeat era at the Cavern. The club was packed full and excited people danced to the music. Bob Wooler christened Rory 'The Golden Boy' and 'Mr Show Business' for his onstage antics. One even included him jumping from the stage into the crowd and body-surfing as the hands of those watching held him up. Nobody else was doing anything like that. Ray may have loved Jazz, but he knew that Rock 'n' Roll was the way forward.

At the Jive Hive on 6 April, the band decided to all wear sunglasses and palm tree shirts. They also brought along a washboard and treated

Rory on stage at Butlins. The girl dancing in front of him while looking back towards the camera is his sister Iris. (Courtesy of Iris Caldwell)

the crowd to a couple of skiffle numbers. It went down brilliant to huge cheers, showing once more that they were not afraid to try anything to please a crowd. The Hurricanes joined the Musician's Union before going to Butlins on 4 June. You can see just how serious they were taking it all. Suits were ordered from Duncan the Tailors – bright blue for Rory and pinky red for the band. These guys liked to stand out. The local press were, of course, called to snap them wearing the suits outside the shop.

At the holiday camp they had three rooms between five of them. Johnny and Lou shared, as did Ringo and Ty. Rory had a chalet to himself, and was very happy about it. They started to use their stage names all the time at Butlins, and Ringo was given his own slot – 'Starr Time' – where he would sing 'Boys' or 'Alley Oop'. They stood out in their brightly coloured suits; they were different and they knew it. Rory would introduce each member of the band, who would then play a solo on their instrument.

The stage in the Rock 'n' Calypso Ballroom had a piano at the rear directly behind Ringo's drum kit. Rory would climb up on it and begin to shake, before leaping through the air right over Ringo's head. The holidaymakers loved them, Butlins loved them, and the girls loved them. The guys received plenty of attention from the females who arrived every week. They were young and enjoying their life as Butlins stars. Rory even pretended that his birthday was in July so that he could celebrate it at

A beach party after the night's show at Butlins. Lou is playing guitar while Johnny and Ringo fool around and Rory gives a wave. (Courtesy of Walter Eymond)

Butlins with the holidaymakers, or in reality with the girls. He knocked a couple of years off his age to appear younger – he was only twenty-two anyway. You just have to laugh at his crazy ideas at times. The season proved a huge success for The Hurricanes. It toned them up and gave them a cutting-edge.

Rory's sister Iris was working in Butlins at the same time as the band. Being very pretty, she attracted the attention of a lot of the guys there, but Rory was having none of it. If he saw a lad chatting to her he would go over and tell him that he had better not see his hands moving or else, driving would-be pursuers away. However, Iris did have a brief romance with Ty – nothing serious, just a few dates. He would sing 'Ive told every little star just how sweet I think you are, why haven't I told you' to her. Linda Scott had a huge hit with this song in 1961.

While at Butlins, the lads would spend a lot of time during the day around the pool area. Rory was a terrific swimmer, showing off his dives from the high diving platform to the holidaymakers. Double twists, back flips, he could do them all, with perfect landings into the water. Ringo would sit around sunbathing, ignoring the others' pleas for him to get into the pool. One day he explained to Ty and Lou that he could not swim and that he was embarrassed by it. They told him they would teach him, and after getting him into the pool he took to it well.

Above: Rory at Butlins.
(Courtesy of Iris Caldwell)

Right: The lads after a
performance at Butlins
Eileen is sitting on Johnny.
Notice Ty, who was getting
changed, popping his
head out for the picture.
(Courtesy of Walter
Eymond)

The guys would often host parties on the Pwllheli beach after the evening's events at the holiday camp had ended. In the day they would go to the beach and dig a large hole for people to sit in as protection from the wind, before collecting wood for a fire. Crates of beer were purchased, while bacon, sausage and other food items were acquired (most often from the Butlins kitchens). After their show guests would be invited, and they all made their way to the beach, lit a fire, and shared the food, beer and a few songs.

They returned to Liverpool on 4 September and had a two-week break that included a trip to London. In the capital city's nightclubs they found the girls rather unwelcoming towards the boys from up North, a few times being told to 'fuck off' when asking a girl for a dance. Local promoter Allan Williams had made a contact with Bruno Koschmider, a German club owner in Hamburg. They had agreed that

Rory pictured at Butlins with his sister Iris sitting side-on in the front chair. (Courtesy of Iris Caldwell)

Williams would supply Liverpool bands to play at the Indra and the Kaiserkeller clubs in the St Pauli area of Hamburg. Derry and The Seniors had already signed with Bruno to play at the Kaiserkeller, and he told Williams he wanted another group. Allan asked The Hurricanes, but they had the Butlins booking over the summer and they would not give it up. He then asked Gerry and The Pacemakers who also turned him down. Finally he sent out The Beatles, driving them there himself. They began a two-month spell at the Indra club in August 1960. The Hurricanes had agreed to go out later in the year, and they were booked to replace The Seniors at the Kaiserkeller from 1 October to 31 December. Of course they made sure that they were paid more money than the other groups.

Rory's mother Vi was not happy about the band playing in Germany: 'Why does it have to be Germany?' she would ask Rory. Ernie would chip in with 'The German people suffered as well Vi', but she was having none of it, replying 'Thank god all British men are not as sympathetic as you, or Alan and Iris would have been taught German in school.' Vi was still full of anger from the war years and hated the thought of her son singing to those who had bombed her city. She knew Rory would go regardless of her feelings, and warned him that without knowing it he may end up talking to the man who killed his uncle Len.

Following their short break the band played a handful of gigs, including The Cavern and The Jive Hive. Then it was off to Germany, leaving Liverpool by Train and arriving in Holland by boat; Johnny was sick as it sailed. Another long train journey into Germany followed, before their arrival in Hamburg. It was pouring with rain when they came out of the train station and jumped into taxis. On their arrival at the Kaiserkeller club they found it closed; nobody was around and they were standing there with luggage and instruments as the rain fell. They heard music coming from up the street – an English band – and followed the noise to investigate. Just further along the Grosse Freiheit they found the music coming from a club called The Indra. Venturing inside they found a band practicing, and to their amazement it was The Beatles, who they knew from Liverpool. The Hurricanes never played at the Indra, but they did watch The Beatles there a couple of times.

They had to wait for the Kaiserkeller to open. When it did their expectations and excitement were brought down to earth with the news that no sleeping arrangements had yet been made for them. They had to rough it that first night with Derry and The Seniors. When Derry and the band left a few days later The Hurricanes were offered the rooms next to the Kaiserkeller stage. It was a dump, but much better than the hovel that The Beatles were living in at the Bambi Kino cinema. The guys decided to look elsewhere for accommodation and booked into the German Seamen's Mission further along the Reeperbahn.

On 1 October Rory Storm and The Hurricanes took to the stage at the Kaiserkeller. The band did four sets of around ninety minutes each – six hours in total. They finished at 6.00 a.m., exhausted, and fell into bed. They awoke, dressed and had to start playing again. This time they ended at 5 a.m. and once more fell into bed. The Beatles had been playing at the nearby Indra club, but they had to move on 4 October after complaints by neighbours about the noise. Bruno brought them to the Kaiserkeller to perform with The Hurricanes.

The posters at the club listed The Hurricanes as the main act, with The Beatles supporting. This reflected the standings in Liverpool where Rory and the boys were the bigger band. The Beatles also brought pills with them that could help a person stay awake, which were great for the long hours that they had to play. It is not certain if any Hurricanes members used the wakey-wakey pills, but we do know that Rory did not. He would not use any drugs and he very rarely drank. He was an athlete and kept his body in top condition. Tea was his tipple.

While playing together the two groups became friends. The Beatles had admired Rory and The Hurricanes back in Liverpool, and the lads from both bands got along well together. The stage at the Kaiserkeller was rather dated and beginning to rot. The groups noticed a section that was starting to give way and made a bet with each other as to

The stage at The Kaiserkeller club. Part of the stage is still the original that The Hurricanes and Beatles played on in 1960.

which band could break through it. Bruno was impressed to see the two bands jumping around the stage, unaware of their true intentions. A leap by Rory from the top of the piano finally did it, and he disappeared through the floor, followed by most of Ringo's drum kit. The music had to stop while the stage was fixed, and records had to be played to the customers.

Most Beatle books state that both bands went off to a local cafe to celebrate the demise of the stage, and that when Bruno found out he was furious and sent his henchmen after them to give them a beating. However, when this story was put to Walter Eymond he gave the following response:

Utter Rubbish! That never happened. Ourselves and The Beatles went over to Harold's cafe after the stage was broken and nobody came after us. For one thing, we were friends with Horst Fascher who was a very tough guy who had been a professional boxer, so Bruno would have done nothing knowing that Horst and his brother Freddie were pals of us and The Beatles. Second, I would never have put up with that, and Ty certainly would not have. He was a hard lad, as anyone daft enough to take him on would have found out. So, that story is untrue. Bruno's guys would sometimes have a go at us in The Kaiserkeller, but we would tell them where to go. Even Rory, Johnny and Ringo, who tended to avoid any fights would not have put up with that. Neither would John, Paul, George or Stu, and Pete Best was another guy who could handle himself well. Sadly many of the books are extremely fictional at times. Does anyone really believe that the two bands would carry on playing for a club who had sent people to beat them up? The truth is that we both went to Harold's and probably had cornflakes.

There was one occasion when a band member and a bouncer came to blows and it involved Lou Walters. The bouncer was given him a hard time so Lou told him where to go. When the guy threw a punch Lou ducked, before kneeing the guy between the legs then punching him. After that, the bouncers called the musicians 'dirty fighters' and tended to lay off them.

Bruno Koschmider was always shouting at the groups to jump around and perform on stage. 'Mach Schau! Mach Schau!' he would shout at them as he commanded that they 'make a good show'. The Hurricanes and Beatles now played ninety-minute sets each as the music became non-stop. It was tough work, but the long hours playing improved the musical abilities of both bands. Bruno also had another huge problem in Rory, who would go missing when Lou sang or when the band played an instrumental number. He would shout at Rory, telling him to stay on stage, but Rory was Rory, the self-made superstar; he would do as he liked.

Gretal & Alfons bar pictured early 1960s. (Courtesy of Ted Kingsize Taylor)

George Harrison had spotted a Fender Stratocaster guitar for sale and wanted to buy it. Neither he nor the other members of The Beatles had enough money to get it, but Rory did and he told George that he would lend him what he needed. When Johnny found out he told Rory that Ty needed a new guitar and asked 'Why are you lending George the money when Ty needs one?' Rory then gave the cash to Ty and the guitar was his. George was gutted while John Lennon got angry, and there was a bit of mixed feelings. The bad blood between the two bands lasted a few days, but they were soon back to being good mates.

No fight had occurred during the guitar saga, but it almost happened on another occasion. The two groups were sitting around eating when Ty got fed up with John Lennon and his put-down remarks to Stuart. Ty told him to pack it in and leave Stu alone, while John responded by standing up and telling Ty to mind his own business. Ty stood up himself and said 'it is my business now', leaving John in no doubt of his intentions. John was not stupid and knew that Ty was a hard lad with boxing skills, but before he could sit down Paul stood up to back John, to which Lou rose and said 'sit down Paul'. They both did and the situation was defused and friendships resumed. Incidentally, Ty would later sand down the body of the Strat and paint it pale blue.

In the last week of November, things between Rory and Bruno finally came to a head. Bruno had never forgiven Rory for breaking the stage, and had told one of his henchmen to harass the singer. The guy was a bit on the small side, but he pressured as much as he could until his prey snapped back. Enough was enough, and after calling the henchman a 'fucking Nazi dwarf' Rory laid him out with a punch. Lou Walters recalled that it was the first time he had ever seen Rory hit anyone. Bruno sacked him on the spot and demanded that he pay 65 Deutsche Mark for breaking the stage. Rory responded by taking the large advertising poster and Bruno called the police to report him for theft, but with the poster well hidden there was nothing to charge him with. The lads wanted to leave as well, but Rory told them to stay. They continued at the club with Lou taking over lead vocals.

When Rory was sacked he at first had nowhere to stay as Bruno had informed the Seaman's mission that Rory was no longer working. So, the lads from the band told him to just climb through the window of the mission so he was not seen. While clambering through one evening he was spotted, and the person who saw him rang the police to report it. He was in the room when a loud knock came at the door. A terrified Rory hid in the wardrobe as Lou went to answer the door. The police were there and Lou told them 'nobody has broken in here; we are on our way out gents'. As they all walked out of the room a knocking sound could be heard, followed by Rory shouting 'come on lads, stop taking the piss'. The police

The Flurschänke pub pictured left, and to the right the house that stands there today. Rory played here a number of times. (Pub photo courtesy of Thomas Werzinger)

entered the room and opened the wardrobe. Rory fell out onto the floor and the lads all burst out laughing. Rory was taken to the police station, but they let him go and he returned to the Seaman's mission where he climbed back through the window.

Rory found a job at the Top Ten club playing with Tony Sheridan, and stayed there until the end of the year. Rory also played at the Studio X club upstairs from The Kaiserkeller. The Beatles followed Rory to the Top Ten club not long after, but as they had broken their contract with Bruno he put the police onto them. George, Paul, and Pete were deported, John made his own way home, while Stu stayed and moved in with his German girlfriend Astrid Kirchherr, who would later take a stunning and iconic photograph of Rory.

For a short period Tony Sheridan had fallen out with owner of the Top Ten club Peter Eckhorn and went to live and play at a bar called Flurschänke in the Osdorf area of Hamburg, around 5 miles from the Reeprbahn. Rory also played at the pub on a number of occasions and slept there many times.

Gerry and The Pacemakers came over to Hamburg, giving The Hurricanes friends from Liverpool to hang out with. New Year's Eve saw the end of their contract with Koschmider. Rory had found them work at the Flurschänke pub, a much nicer place than the Kaiserkeller. They started on New Year's Day and loved it there. However, Bruno arrived at the club with the contract that they had signed stating they would not play at for another rival for six months after 31 December. The owner of the Flurschänke had no option but to let them go or face legal action. Lou, Ty and Ringo left for home the next day, while Rory and Johnny came two days later. They conned their way home on trains and boats, with Rory managing to make it all the way to Liverpool without paying a single penny. Rory had also lost his passport, but still made it home without it. Johnny was sick on the ferry.

While in Hamburg, Lou had collected a lot of brandy glasses, asking for them at every bar or club that he went into. He had collected quite a lot of them, all in various sizes with ornate designs, and he had them all packed into a box so that he could get them home safely. However, while they were at the Hook of Holland, Lou forgot to take them with him. He boarded the ship back to the UK and never saw the glasses again. Rory had already taken the advertising poster from outside the Kaiserkeller when he was sacked by Bruno. When the lads had finished their contract, Johnny, Ty and Ringo all took a poster as well. We must thank the lads for keeping them safe as they have turned into iconic posters over the years.

Johnny Ball, who later presented the TV show *Think of a Number*, had met the band when he was working as a Red Coat in Butlins. He found a job in Liverpool and lodged at Rory's house, sleeping in Rory's room when the band was in Germany. Rory's sister Iris and her dancer friend Ginny would play jokes on Johnny. He could never get out of bed and Vi would be waiting at the front door with a cup of tea for him while shouting up the stairs to tell him he would be late for work. He would run down and go straight out to catch his bus. Iris and Ginny once sewed up the buttonholes on his coat and watched as he ran out of the house late again and wondered why he could not fasten his coat. Another time they sewed a bra onto the back of his coat and he went to work in it. He could not understand why people kept laughing until he reached his workplace, hung up his coat, and saw the bra. He and Iris still laugh about it.

Allan Williams had come over to Hamburg just after The Hurricanes had arrived, as he wanted to see how they were doing. While there he paid for Lou Walters to record a number of songs with a Mr Breul who ran the akustik studio located in Kirchenalle 57. The recording session was booked for 15 October and its importance in musical history cannot be doubted. Present at the studio, apart from Lou and Williams, were Ty, Johnny and Ringo. Also, there were three members of The Beatles – John, Paul and George. Pete Best had gone on a shopping trip for new drumsticks, while Stuart Sutcliffe was believed to be with his girlfriend Astrid. Rory came to the studio later in the day. Three songs were recorded: 'Summertime', 'Fever' and 'September Song'. Lou played bass, Ty guitar, and Ringo drums on 'Fever' and 'September Song', with Johnny slotting in bits on guitar. The three Beatles, along with Ringo, backed Lou on 'Summertime'. This of course makes that song the first recording by the four Beatles as we know them, an important piece of history, and as Sod's law would have it, no copies of the recording are known to exist; maybe somewhere in a drawer or a box in an attic sits an old 78 disc worth an absolute fortune.

Walter Eymond said, 'The books have the story wrong, Allan did not ask The Beatles to come along as he thought them better than The Hurricanes. He heard me sing and liked my voice, so he asked me if I would record while being backed by The Hurricanes. The Beatles tagged along and we let them stand in to back me on "Summertime" Pete was not there so Ringo played on drums. Rory had a gob on as he was not asked to sing by Allan, but did arrive at the studio to cheer me on. And, that is the real story of the session.'

4

Mates with The Beatles

The day after they returned to Liverpool, the Hurricanes went along to the Litherland Town Hall to watch The Beatles play. Faron Ruffley was there and recalled how the Beatles and Hurricanes greeted each other with hugs and handshakes – after all they had become good friends in Hamburg. Rory had also started running again in the day; his dedication to his fitness was undoubted. The Hurricanes first gig back in their home city was at Mossway Hall in Croxteth on 6 January 1961, followed the next night (Rory's Birthday) at the Alexandra Hall in Crosby. Ty was unwell and had to miss the night in Crosby, along with the next two performances. John Gustafson from The Big Three, who would later play with Roxy Music and the Ian Gillan Band, filled in with them while he was off. Ty was back on the 13 January when they played again at Mossway Hall, before gigs at the Jive Hive and the Cherokee club in Bold Street.

The following week the gigs came thick and fast once more. They were back from Hamburg and the club owners and promoters wanted to book them. January ended with them playing at the Hambleton Hall in St David's Road, Huyton, Aintree Institute, Lathom Hall in Seaforth, Litherland Town Hall, and of course the Jive Hive. The first two weeks of February saw them at venues such as Lowlands in West Derby, Hambleton Hall, Cassanova club on the corner of London Road and Fraser Street, Mossway Hall, Lathom Hall, Aintree Institute, The Rocket, and their old favourite the Jive Hive.

Then came Valentine's Day and a booking at the Cassanova club, playing alongside The Beatles. The two bands were now becoming good friends. The Beatles had improved as a group through the long hours in Hamburg, and had rightfully taken their position as one of the top Liverpool acts. They had looked up to The Hurricanes in the past, and now the respect was mutual. Promoters wanted to book both bands, so their paths were crossing and they were hanging out together. They would come to watch each other play, go to parties, or sit in one of the late-night cafés together. The Beatles had admired how The Hurricanes moved about on stage and asked the lads if would teach them a few routines. Lou Walters recalled the episode with laughter: 'They were hopeless, and John Lennon had more than two left feet.'

Another popular place to hang out was at Rory's house in Broad Green Road, where everyone was welcome and the house usually full. Violet was a night owl and would treat her son's friends to chip butties, cheese barms and an endless supply of tea. Ernie, in bed upstairs, would often shout down 'stop using my electric'. The Beatles affectionalty called Violet 'Violent Vi' and Ernie 'The Crusher'.

Many members of other bands would also visit the house, with Cilla Black and Bob Wooler being regulars. Bob called Vi 'Ma Storm'. Vi would have everyone rolling in laughter with her comments and blunt criticism, which could bring the biggest ego down to earth. She would organise silly games for them all, even performing a séance one night with Paul, George and Cilla. Everybody loved Vi, and Paul and George were very close to her. The guitars would come out for a sing-song, which would sometimes cause the neighbours to bang on the walls and for Ernie to shout from upstairs "I have to be up for work in the morning.'

We can only guess as to how amazing it must have been to sit in that house with all the musicians playing crazy games. Those who were there speak of it with great fondness and say that there was nowhere else like it. It is perhaps a little shocking that the present-day Beatles tours in Liverpool do not stop at the house, as it does, after all, hold such history to The Beatles, Hurricanes and the Liverpool music scene.

Ernie was also prone to the odd bout of sleepwalking, and with the house being full most of the time people saw him, though nobody would dare to wake him. The next day they would tell him about it and he would brush it off and tell them they were just trying to kid him. One night he came downstairs dressed in pyjamas and clearly sleepwalking. Everyone held their hands over their mouths to muffle their giggles, and then a huge shock: Ernie walked out of the front door. Everyone was stunned as he was still asleep. Paul McCartney ran after him and followed him as he walked all the way around Oakhill Park and back to the house. Paul had taken a camera with him and snapped Ernie walking the streets in his pyjamas. We have no idea if Paul ever showed him the photos, or what Ernie's reaction was.

Rory, ever the egomaniac, changed the name of his family home. Most books and almost everyone you talk with will tell you that the house was called 'stormsville', while Cavern DJ Bob Wooler had insisted that the house was in fact christened 'Hurricaneville'. A check of the phone books up to 1971 will show you that listed as the bill payer is Rory Storm, address Hurricaneville, Broad Green Road 13, phone number Stoneycroft

9517, though people are adamant that it was called Stormsville. Did he first call it Hurricaneville then adopt Stormsville, leaving the phone book address unchanged?

The Hurricanes continued to play to a busy schedule at the venues already listed, plus a night at the Bowaters paper mill social club in Little Sutton in Ellsemere Port. On 6 March they played at the Liverpool Jazz Society in Temple Street, otherwise known as The Iron Door. The event was called 'Rocking Good Time Tonight' and on the bill with The Hurricanes were The Beatles, Derry and The Seniors, Gerry and The Pacemakers, and Kingsize Taylor and The Dominoes. The Beatles had opened with a great show, followed by Gerry and The Pacemakers, who also had the crowd worked up. Next on where The Hurricanes, and Rory knew he needed to turn up the performance to match the other two bands. They did their set and had the place bouncing. Then Rory chose his moment and with a huge leap he cleared the piano and Ringo's drum kit before bursting into 'Roll Over Beethoven'. The girls who were packing the front of the stage all jumped up in shock as Rory landed in front of them from nowhere, then the place went crazy. Rory had done it again. The next day Rory, Johnny and Ringo went along

The original tiled doorstep at No. 54 Broad Green Road. So many famous people have walked on this.

to the afternoon session at The Iron Door. Lou and Ty were at their day jobs, so when offered a slot during the session they recruited two more members, Derek Bond from The Seniors joined them on bass, while a guy named Paul McCartney played piano. Calling themselves 'Rory Storm and The Wild Ones', they played nine afternoon sessions at the club in the following weeks, sometimes with different members, with John Lennon and George Harrison believed to have joined in at one point.

The Iron Door was proving to be a popular venue with the public and was packing them in. On 11 March they ran an all night Rock Ball. On the bill with The Hurricanes were The Beatles, The Remo Four, Kingsize Taylor and The Dominoes, The Big Three, Derry and The Seniors, Gerry and The Pacemakers, Dale Roberts and The Jaywalkers, The Pressmen, Johnny Rocco and The Jets, and Faron and The Tempest Tornadoes. It proved a popular event, with two more nights being set for a weekend at the end of March. The Beatles did not play these dates, having by then returned to Hamburg.

14 March again saw the band playing at the Iron Door club. Rory had just come off stage as Lou took the microphone to sing 'Fever'. As he did a girl he knew named Pat was shouting 'let her sing' at him from the front row while pointing at her friend. Lou then asked the girl named Cilla if she would like to get up and sing. She agreed, and went down well with the audience. She later went on to find fame as Cilla Black, so you could

The Hurricanes at the Iron Door. (Courtesy of Iris Caldwell)

say that Lou Walters played his part in starting her career. Cilla sang with the band on a number of occasions afterwards.

Before March was out, The Institute in Neston and the music hall in Shrewsbury had been added to their engagements to play that month. Along with their regular venues, they had also returned to The Casbah in West Derby. On 29 March The Hurricanes auditioned in Garston for another summer season at Butlins, passing with flying colours and being booked to start there in June. The Hurricanes' gigs started to expand out of the city during April and May of 1961, with performances at The Institute in Neston, The Queen's Hall in Widnes, The Majestic Ballroom in Crewe, and the Ballroom between the swings and helter-skelter at the Mersey View Pleasure Grounds in Frodsham. They had also begun playing at the Knotty ash village hall in Liverpool. They played the Crewe gig on 27 May. Afterwards, they went to Cilla Black's house on Scotland Road for her eighteenth birthday party.

The Hurricanes now prepared for their second season at Butlins in Pwllheli, buying new outfits, the louder the better in Rory's case. Glam Rock had come a decade early for this guy. Rory had once asked his mother what jacket looked best on him, a green one or a bright orange one? Vi chose the orange jacket. Rory returned home in the early hours saying 'cheers for that mum' after the customers in the Catholic club had thrown anything they could get their hands on at him for wearing that colour. Rory however could turn most situations into a performance, and as the crowd threw their objects he sang 'don't throw bouquets at me, throw tables and chairs'. Butlins proved another success, with them giving the holidaymakers some great entertainment.

They made it back to Liverpool in July for Ringo's twenty-first birthday, where over sixty people packed into the tiny living room at his house in Admiral Grove. Many of the names from the Liverpool music scene where there, including Gerry and The Pacemakers, Cilla Black and of course The Hurricanes. The Beatles however, were not present. The long season at Butlins had firmed them up to be a great band worth watching. Rory of course was as crazy as ever, the perfect frontman. Butlins wanted them back the following year, next time at Skegness.

Being the house band, the Hurricanes were picked as judges for the talent contests that were held for the holidaymakers. Of course they ensured that any friends of theirs won the prizes on offer. They also bunked a few people into the holiday camp, including Cilla Black who they threw over the fence to get in. They had told Cilla and Bobby Thomson to get up and sing in the talent contest, ensuring them they would win. This of course they did, and they awaited their prizes. A Butlins official arrived on stage with the prizes, first presenting one to Bobby Thomson, congratulating him and asking for his chalet number, which Bobby duly gave. He then turned to Cilla who said 'I don't want the prize', before running off the

Rory enjoying free time at Butlins by horse riding. (Courtesy of Iris Caldwell)

stage and keeping her secret from the official that she was not supposed to be there. On many other occasions the winners of the talents contests turned out to be friends of the members of the band.

The group were booked to play aboard the *Royal Iris* ferry for one of the Beat shows. The Hurricanes, alongside other groups, were loading their gear onto the *Royal Iris* when Rory drove up and just climbed on the bonnet of his car and started sunbathing. It was nearing sailing time and Rory was still lying on the bonnet of his car. The ferry started to move and the others all shouted 'come on Rory, we are sailing'. Rory jumped off his car as he saw the ferry move. He started to run, before producing an almighty athletic leap that landed him on the boat's rails, from where he climbed up. All the groups and everybody else looked on in amazement, not in awe of his fantastic leap across the water to the boat, but because he had jumped on the wrong ferry – yes indeed, Rory had managed to land aboard the Isle of Man ferry.

The Hurricanes returned to Liverpool still a major crowd-puller, and the club owners were eager to book them. The Orrell Park Ballroom, the Jive Hive, and Litherland Town Hall happened alongside gigs further afield in Northwich, St Helens, and Ellesmere Port. They also returned to the Majestic Ballroom in Crewe on 4 November, travelling there in the band's van. Johnny had brought fireworks and thought it would be great fun to set them off from the moving vehicle. He faced the wrath of Ty who was furious with him for being so stupid.

Rory at Butlins with Johnny's and Lou's guitars. (Courtesy of Iris Caldwell)

On 20 October 1961 The Hurricanes played the Memorial Hall in Shrewsbury, on the same bill as Emile Ford. They were booked to play two sets with Emile performing first. Emile opened the show and Rory went nuts saying, 'He is stealing me show.' Jamo told him not to worry and to just go out there and steal it back. Rory chose to bide his time until the band played their last set, then chose his moment to steal the show by leaping onto a piano before climbing up to the balcony. The crowd went crazy and the girls rushed the stage. Rory lost his grip and fell straight through the piano. As he tried to climb out he was mobbed by the adoring ladies, and although he had splinters of wood sticking out of his leg he was more worried about the girls tearing his gold lame shirt.

Ringo was outside having a smoke after the gig when he was approached by three lads and an argument started. Jamo heard Ringo saying 'you couldn't survive where I live so don't fucking start', then he noticed Ty and Lou running down the steps taking off their watches – a sure sign of a scuffle, as Jamo well knew. It was all smoothed over without any real trouble and the lads headed off with Emile Ford to a coffee bar. At the bar Emile took a brush and painted 'EMILE FORD AND THE CHECKMATES' on the wall, before telling The Hurricanes to write their names alongside it. When they had, Rory told Jamo to add his name and he replied 'there is no room', before taking the brush and writing his name in huge letters on another wall. A short while later Jamo, Ringo, Johnny and Ty were all in the toilets talking about the minor scuffle outside the memorial hall when Lou burst in and shouted 'Quick lads, you gotta see this.' they all came out to see Rory up a ladder painting over Jamo's name and shouting 'I am not having your name bigger than mine.'

The Tower Ballroom, New Brighton. (Photographer unattributed. Courtesy and permission from the collection at Wallasey Central Reference Library)

Local promoter Sam Leach had already booked The Hurricanes, along with other local bands in Liverpool. He had also hit upon the idea of getting the big groups to play together on the same bill, though the popularity of these gigs left him with another problem: he needed to find a larger venue to host them. The Tower Ballroom in New Brighton proved ideal and on 10 November 1961 'Operation Big Beat' took place. The Beatles, Gerry and The Pacemakers, Kingsize Taylor and The Dominoes, and The Remo Four joined Rory Storm and The Hurricanes on the stage at the Tower Ballroom. It was a huge success, with almost 5,000 people paying to watch the bands on show. Sam recalled how when dealing with Rory over a price for performing, Rory's stutter would get worse: 'I am sure he was doing it on purpose', said Sam. 'He would ask for £12 and I would offer £10, then he would stutter like crazy. In the end I would tell him have the £12 then.'

The Hurricanes and The Beatles then had a van race back to Rory's house in Liverpool. Coming through the Mersey tunnel, Rory and the boys almost smashed head-on into an approaching car. Taking the sharp corner at the bottom of Upper Parliament Street in Liverpool, Jamo almost turned over the Hurricanes' van. It was dangerous and stupid stuff, but they all managed to get back safely for chip butties and tea with Vi. As they all laughed back in Rory's house, Ringo informed them that he had

At Butlins with the family. Johnny with Eileen and his mum Elsie, then Johnny's brother's Pat and Paul. Rory with his mum Vi and his sister Iris at the front with her friend Wendy. (Courtesy of Iris Caldwell)

once again applied to go to Texas. The guys looked on shocked; Ringo was getting the urge to move on.

Rory cut an imposing figure on stage – 6 foot 2 inches, blonde, blue-eyed and good looking. The girls swooned for him, while the lads, though green with envy, admired him. He was the ultimate showman, always surprising and ready to attempt something crazy. He could grasp an audience and control them, and was impressive out front where he ruled the stage. In November of 1961, Brian Epstein descended the steps of The Cavern club and saw The Beatles perform. It was the start of something big for them, with one person later saying 'If he had seen Rory Storm and The Hurricanes first, then The Beatles would have been staying in Liverpool playing the circuit.' To be fair though, The Beatles had proved how talented they were.

The Hurricanes played a gig at the Holyoake Hall on Smithdown Road. Rory was his usual flamboyant self and was really going down well with the girls who had crowded around the stage. This had annoyed most of their boyfriends, and of course Rory revelled in it. The lads began to threaten Rory and told him that they would get him outside. They all congregated around the stage door waiting to beat him to a pulp. One guy was trying to calm them down, saying 'come on lads it's his act, he doesn't mean any harm, he is just a showman, but the lads were having none of it. Next thing the door swung open and Rory ran out wearing his running shorts, legging it down the road tailed by all these lads trying to catch him.

24 November saw part two of 'Operation Big Beat', and again it proved a great success. Alongside The Hurricanes were The Beatles, The Remo Four, Gerry and The Pacemakers, Faron Young and The Flamingos, and Earl Preston and The Tempest Tornadoes. Two surprise guests were the singer Emile Ford, who sang 'Fever' and 'Hound Dog', backed by The Hurricanes, while The Beatles supported Davy Jones. After the show, Rory asked Ringo why would he want America when he has all these screaming fans to play for. Ringo flipped out, shouting 'I come from a rough shithole, not the nice suburbs like you lot, life is hard, why should I be happy.' Ty took offence and told him to shut up. Ringo called him an arsehole and the two guys almost came to blows before they were separated by their bandmates.

A couple more dates with The Beatles at The Tower Ballroom took place before Sam Leach came up with the idea of a Liverpool *v* London battle of the bands; the venue was to be The Palais Ballroom in Aldershot. The Beatles travelled down with Sam for the first of three Saturday night gigs. Sam had arranged for the London band Ivor Jay and The Jaywalkers to also play that first night. The press had been invited along, as had a number of London record producers. They arrived expecting big things, but walked into an empty hall. The Jaywalkers had not turned up; neither had any record producers or press. In fact, only eighteen paying members of the public had bothered to come along. It was a complete failure, though The Beatles still played to the tiny crowd. Back in Liverpool Sam told Rory that they may as well cancel as the place was no good.

Lou singing at the New Brighton Pavilion. (Courtesy of Walter Eymond)

Rory was having none of it and insisted that they play, plus he wanted paying whether they did or not. The following Saturday they rocked the ballroom to a sell-out crowd. What a difference a week makes ...

Ringo told the band that he wanted to take up an offer from Tony Sheridan to join him at the Top Ten club in Hamburg. He explained that it was only for a couple of months and that he would return to them afterwards. The Hurricanes would not stand in his way if that was what he really wanted, and they told him that he would be welcomed back. Ringo was with them on the drums when they played the 'Boxing Night Ball' at New Brighton's Tower Ballroom. The guys then went along and waved him off from Lime Street station on 30 December with the best of wishes. Derek Fell was brought in as a temporary replacement on drums.

Ringo set off for Hamburg under great excitement. The Top Ten club was a far more upmarket club than the Kaiserkeller, plus he had his own flat. Life would be good. Ringo however soon grew tired of Tony changing songs without warning, and packed it in to return to Liverpool. The Hurricanes were glad to have him back, but Ringo was showing enough signs of restlessness for them to become a little worried.

The *Mersey Beat* music paper, run and edited by Bill Harry, delivered the results of its poll for Liverpool's top band on 4 January 1962. The Beatles came first, Gerry and The Pacemakers second, The Remo Four third, with Rory Storm and the Hurricanes coming in fourth place. Rory went mad, calling the results 'total bullshit'. In fact The Hurricanes had come first in the poll, but had been placed fourth after a number of their entries had been found to be written in the same pen, with the same handwriting. Other bands had clearly cheated, buying many copies of the paper to use the entry forms. The Beatles even admitted that they had cheated themselves. The lads in the band felt angry as it was just them who had been docked votes.

In Liverpool, The Hurricanes and Beatles continued to join each other on a number of bills, including the Tower Ballroom and the Floral Hall in Southport. There was no animosity between the two bands over the Merseybeat poll. They remained the best of friends, even helping each other out during gigs. Ringo sat in with The Beatles when Pete Best was ill, while Rory took the place of John Lennon when he came down with laryngitis. On 24 January 1962, The Beatles signed a contract with Brian Epstein that made him their manager. Everyone was expecting Rory and the boys to be snapped up in no time at all.

The two bands played a memorable night together at the Knotty Ash Village Hall on 17 March – St Patrick's Night, or as they say in Liverpool, 'Paddy's Night'. The hall had been hired by Sam Leach to celebrate his engagement, with The Beatles and Hurricanes being only too happy to perform. Both bands played out of their skins, treating the partygoers to a real thumping taste of Merseybeat. They ended the night by forming a

Rory and Lou on stage at Butlins. (Courtesy of Iris Caldwell)

nine-strong supergroup for an extended version of 'Honey Don't'. It was incredible, and those there loved it, what a performance from two of the best groups in Liverpool. But what would the supergroup have been called? Beatcanes or Hurricles? Afterwards, it was all back to a house party to continue the celebrations, where Rory allowed himself a few drinks. As he was usually teetotal, he was soon drunk, slouching on the couch to enjoy the remainder of the party.

Near the end of March, Ringo sat in with The Beatles for a couple of gigs while Pete Best was ill. After a few days John, Paul and George made noises about Ringo joining their band. Soon the two groups would be off on their travels – The Hurricanes to France and The Beatles to Germany. They were also about to travel in very different directions musically, with an event later in the year changing their friendship forever.

Paul McCartney had noticed a stunning-looking girl dancing one night in 1961, when The Beatles were playing at The Tower Ballroom in New Brighton. He could not take his eyes off her and ended up going over to chat to her. As he asked her name she replied, 'Paul, it's me, Iris Caldwell.' Paul was stunned that this was Rory's little sister? Iris, now seventeen, had been hired to perform the twist at the ballroom. Already a natural beauty, she looked even more amazing dressed up and dancing. They soon began dating, though Iris forgot to mention that she was also dating the singer Frank Ifield.

The importance of Rory's mother Vi to everyone who met her was demonstrated by The Beatles' continued correspondence with her even after they had hit the big time; often they would phone her up for a chat. One evening, after making one of their early TV appearances, George phoned Vi to ask her what she thought of it. She was as blunt as ever, telling him that they were OK but they needed to smile. The next time they were on TV George gave a big smile to the camera then rang Vi to ask if that was better. She replied, 'Yes, now tell the others to do it or you will not get anywhere.' George had also sent postcards to Vi when the group were in Hamburg. The Beatles continued to visit the house on Broad Green Road after they had found fame. Paul was still coming to the house until at least 1970. He would visit his father on The Wirral, then drive over to Broad Green in an old battered Morris Minor while wearing a hat or glasses so as not to be recognised. George came many times as well, and he once brought along Pattie Boyd. When Pattie was using the toilet, George asked Vi what she thought of her and she told him she was nice.

One day Ernie was in bed after a night shift at the hospital. Rory was out, and Vi had gone to the shops. Ernie was woken by a knock on the door and opened the bedroom window to see who it was. Standing there were three guys: Paul, George and someone else. Two Beatles were taking their chances by standing outside the house in the daytime, and if noticed by anyone it could have been a nightmare for them. Ernie however, had never been star-struck by anyone and asked them what they wanted. They told him they had come to see Ma Storm and Ernie replied, 'She is at the shops in Old Swan', before going back to bed and leaving them standing there. The two Beatles could not go walking around a busy shopping area so they headed off. Ernie told Vi about them calling later that day and she went mad saying 'Why did you not let them in?' Ernie replied, 'I needed my sleep.'

Rory's friend Pete Vernon recalled him talking about the visits: 'Rory would often come to my house on a Saturday night to watch Match of the day on TV. He would say, "Guess who was in our house on Thursday?" and would go on to say that Paul or George had been around for a visit.' It clearly shows the fondness that they had for the Caldwell family, and maybe it was a way for them to experience a normal life for a few hours during those crazy times of being Beatles?

5

The Year It All Changed

By early 1962, Lou had become fed up with Rory's refusal to learn new material. He, along with Ty and Johnny, was always telling Rory they needed to change the set-up and maybe even consider writing a few songs themselves. When Howie Casey asked Lou if he wanted to join The Seniors to record and play in London he jumped at the chance. Although upset at the thought of losing Lou, The Hurricanes wished him well before looking for a new bass player. An agreement was reached with Kingsize Taylor and The Dominoes, with their bass player Bobby Thomson joining The Hurricanes for their booking in France.

Lou travelled to London with The Seniors, taking his girlfriend Yoelande with him. The band consisted of Howie Casey, Derry Wilkie, Brian Griffiths, Freddie Starr, Frank Wibberly, and of course Lou. They played at the Talk Of The Town club in Ilford, where Lou was approached one night by a rather posh gentleman who told him that he had heard him sing and would like to record him. It was all going so well until the guy told Lou that he could record him in a studio alongside his orchestra. 'Orchestra?' said Lou. 'I'm a Rock 'n' Roll man,' and with that Lou trotted off and left George Martin sitting alone.

Lou and the lads from the band were all in The Black Rose club in Soho one night sitting at a table with Sid James, Adam Faith and Cliff Richard. Lou recalled that while they were sitting there a guy walked in who seemed to put the fear into everyone around him. He was soon followed by another man who looked just as fearsome and the lads watched as they went over to bloke sitting alone who left with them after a quick chat. The band and their party sitting around the table had just set eyes on the Kray twins.

At the end of May 1962, The Hurricanes were ready to leave for France for an engagement at a number of American military bases. The Remo Four had also been engaged and were already playing over in France. A change to the line-up was the addition of a female singer. This had been insisted on by the US military, and they wanted her to be blonde. Vicki Woods, a young girl who sang on the Merseyside social club scene as part of a duo with her mother was hired to sing with The Hurricanes. She would perform a few numbers with them each night. Now they were ready to travel to France. Ringo and Bobby Thomson were sent on ahead by train, with the others driving over in a car.

Ringo and Bobby took the train on 30 March to London, then to Dover, before crossing to Calais. Here, they boarded a train to Bordeaux on their way to Fontenet, just outside St Jean D'Angeley in the south-west of the country. As the train arrived in Paris they were escorted off by armed police who were suspicious of what was in the drum cases. A few days earlier terrorists had exploded a number of bombs in the city, so the drum cases needed searching. They were held up for a long time, and when the police were happy that they held no threat, they were released to carry on their travel. The last train to Bordeaux had already left by then, so they had to book into a hotel in Paris until the next day.

Rory, Johnny, Ty, and Vicki left Liverpool on 31 March. Driving down south for the channel crossing, (Johnny was sick on the boat again) then through France to Fontenet. They arrived almost an hour before Ringo and Bobby, who were not best pleased with their treatment in Paris. They all booked into the Carmine hotel for the first night, before transferring the following day to the much nicer Petite Bar for the remainder of their stay. The group performed at the EM club (Enlisted Members) for the military personnel. The American's loved them, and they loved the

The lads pictured in France. (Courtesy of Iris Caldwell)

US base. They had use of a bowling alley, cinema, and a snack bar. It was like a holiday to them with the goodies at the base and their trips to the beach.

The band had a brilliant month here, and the US soldiers gave them a great send-off on their final night. There had been no women for them to flirt with at the base, but none of that mattered, for it had been great fun and basically a blokes' holiday, with Vicki being treated as one of the lads. The group had also managed to play a gig in a nightclub in Marbella, Spain. It was here that Ringo got into trouble while in the sea and Rory jumped in to save him. They left Fontenet on 30 April and headed off to another base that housed GIs from Orleans. Here, they again received a great reception, with the crowd dancing away and cheering them. On the third night the committee members informed them that they had to stop playing as they were too loud. The GIs liked them, and after getting together a petition the band was allowed to carry on. They were even offered a lengthy contract at the base, but they had arranged to return home and had the Butlins season coming up.

One interesting story to emerge from their time at the EM club in Fontenet was that of John Lennon and Paul McCartney, who are believed to have arrived at the base to talk to Ringo. It is also believed by some that they offered him the job as The Beatles drummer during these talks. Many books will tell you that this meeting never happened, and the author of this book has no idea at all as to whether such an event took place or not. A lot of ex-GIs from the base have mentioned seeing Lennon and McCartney turn up while Ringo was there – Can they all really be

The guys during the tour of France. (Courtesy of Iris Caldwell)

Rory and Johnny pose on the car outside the amphitheatre at Saintes in France. (Courtesy of Iris Caldwell)

mistaken? – yet no Hurricane member has ever confirmed this. They returned to Liverpool, and yes Johnny was sick again on the channel ferry. Then, it was off home for a short rest, a few gigs and the preparations for Butlins. Bobby Thomson stayed to play with The Hurricanes for the season in Skegness.

When Rory had returned home from France, his sister Iris had some dreadful news for him. The Beatles had flown out to Hamburg to begin a stint at the newly opened Star-Club. Waiting for them on their arrival had been Astrid Kirchherr, fiance of Stuart Sutcliffe. She was there to inform them that Stuart had passed away on 10 April after suffering a brain hemorrhage. Rory felt so saddened by the loss of the quiet ex-Beatle who loved to discuss the great painters, a terrible loss at such a young age. Rory also discovered that The Beatles had signed a contract to record an album. He was delighted for them, as were the other members of the band. Their friends had a great chance of making it big.

The Hurricanes left for Butlins, Skegness, on 1 June. Johnny's long-time girlfriend Eileen had found herself a job at the holiday resort so that they could now spend the summer together. Rory's mother Vi also came out for a holiday while they were here. The band once more went down well with the holidaymakers, who danced along and looked on amazed at the antics of the crazy frontman. At the pool they lazed, with the girls they flirted; life was good and they were being paid well. The camp was a hive

Rory posing in France. (Courtesy of Iris Caldwell)

of activity from morning to night, a real entertaining family holiday. The children loved having so much to do, from swimming, games, shows and rides on Gertie the elephant.

One night while the band performed on stage a huge fight broke out. Rory pleaded for calm, while Johnny cursed them under his breath. Unfortunately his words were picked up by the microphone and transmitted to those fighting, a number of whom then turned their attentions on the group members. Ty, Ringo and Bobby escaped, while Rory and Johnny were chased by a mob. A train was coming past the camp so Rory used his athletic skills to outwit his pursuers. He sped up and leapt in front of the moving train, blocking himself off from the mob and leaving them looking on stunned. Johnny still had his mob chasing him, and soon they had him cornered by the south pool. He had no option but to jump in to evade a beating. The mob burst out laughing as he splashed into the water, before walking away and leaving him there. Johnny cared nothing about getting wet as it was better than a beating. As he moved towards the edge of the pool he felt something strange brush his hand; he could also smell an awful odour. Climbing out, he walked back dripping wet, before meeting a member of staff. After Johnny had explained what had happened the man looked at him rather funny and asked him if he was certain that it was the south pool? He was, and the guy then informed him that Gertie the elephant had fallen over and died in that pool that very morning from a heart attack. He went on: 'The crane they brought in to get her out was not strong enough, so they have left her there until a larger one arrives tomorrow.' Johnny was horrified and worried he may have caught a disease. Thankfully he was fine, unlike poor Gertie.

Eileen was sacked when she was found asleep in Johnny's chalet. The group was called to the manager's office as it was against the camp rules

The guys in France.

to have females stay with them. The manager wanted to sack them there and then, but Rory talked him round. It was agreed that they could continue playing, but that Johnny had to live outside the camp and Eileen had to go back to Liverpool. A caravan nearby was hired for him, with Eileen returning to join him there soon after. These guys never did learn to follow rules. Ringo also moved into the caravan with the happy couple.

Ringo received news by letter from The Dominoes that they wanted him as their drummer, the offer was £20 per week. They were happy for him to stay on at Butlins if he joined them on his return to Liverpool. The Seniors had tried to poach Ringo in the past, and he had served a stint with Tony Sheridan in Hamburg. The Hurricanes already had an idea that he wanted out and that he saw his future elsewhere. Ringo decided he would join the Dominoes on his return, his end as a Hurricane was coming. A knock on the caravan door early in the morning of 15 August was answered by Johnny, who found John Lennon and Paul McCartney outside. They wanted to talk with Ringo, who appeared, and they offered him the Beatles drumming job, plus £25 a week. Ringo agreed, but wanted to find Rory to discuss it. The Hurricanes knew it was a waste of time trying to talk around Ringo, his mind was made up. The Beatles had a recording contract, they could not match that.

Rory asked John and Paul if they had told Pete Best that Ringo was taking his job. They told him that Brian Epstein was going to tell him. Rory thought that was a wimp's way out and that they should have told Pete themselves. The Hurricanes also thought that the way they had gone about recruiting Ringo was a bit underhand. Ringo showed no shock at the offer; it was clear that he already had an idea about their intentions. Rory was a big one for talking things through with people if he had a problem or wanted something from them. He was an open book and an honest bloke. He and his bandmates would have preferred their friends to have been open with them from the start, after all the outcome would still have been the same.

The Hurricanes still had a couple of weeks left at Butlins and made this clear to John, Paul and Ringo, telling them 'You are leaving us in the shit.' Ringo agreed to stay for two more nights while they looked for a stand-in drummer. Then he was off, making his debut as a Beatle on 18 August at Hulme Hall in Port Sunlight. The Hurricanes played a couple of nights with a fill-in drummer before they found a guy who said he would play with them for the last few weeks of their contract. He was an actor who also played the drums called Anthony Ashdown, who had appeared in the film *The Loneliness of the Long Distance Runner*. He had also been the band leader and drummer for Gene Vincent until his death. Anthony recalled his time as a Hurricane:

I had gone to Butlins to visit a girlfriend who was with the rep theatre in Butlins Skegness. Being a musician as well as an actor I spent a lot of time in the rock ballroom listening to Rory and the Hurricanes.

I jammed with them a few times, and when Ringo left a lad took over, but Rory asked me to go back to London and get my drums and join them, so I did. They were great, the musicians were excellent, a rarity in those days. Johnny and Ty were not only great musicians, but great company. As was Bobby Thomson who had stood in on bass to replace Lou Walters. I did not stay with them after Butlins as I was working a lot as an actor in London, but I kept in touch with Rory by phone and made the occasional visit to Liverpool. Rory used to joke when I rang him from London about his stammer. He said "you had better take out a mortgage to pay for your phone bill". His mum was great, she fed us and was always very friendly.

A slight Hurricanes connection was made when Anthony played the part of Lieutenant Boyden in the 1967 film *Tobruk*. Rory's uncle Len had been injured while fighting at Tobruk during the Second World War, and that event had led to his death.

Butlins informed the band that their contract would not be renewed. It had nothing to do with Ringo's departure as is claimed at times, and it was nothing to do with their performance after Ringo had gone. They still rocked Butlins and thrilled the crowds for those last few weeks, as many people who saw them still mention. If anything, Johnny's events with Eileen earlier in the holiday season could have been the cause. It had upset the manager and almost resulted in the groups sacking. Back home in Liverpool, it was suggested that Rory should ask Pete Best if he would consider joining them, so he went to see him. Pete's mother told Rory that he was too upset to consider any bands at that moment, so Rory left him alone.

Bobby Thomson returned to The Dominoes while Gibson Kemp joined the Hurricanes on drums as the band began to regroup. Gibson recalled his time of joining: 'I was 16 years old and had been playing music with my mates, then I found myself behind the drums with one of the biggest bands in Liverpool. It was all so exciting. Rory was a first-class performer and the guys were all good lads.' While playing at the Tower Ballroom in New Brighton, Rory spotted Lou Walters in the audience. He went over to him and asked him if he had his bass with him. When Lou replied that he did not Rory said, 'Well what are you going to play then?' to which Lou replied, 'That one on stage.' As simple as that Lou was a Hurricane again.

A number of gigs were booked alongside The Beatles who now had Ringo on drums. Their friendship was still there and The Hurricanes were happy for Ringo, and The Beatles were still visitors to Rory's house for chip butties and tea with Vi. The two bands played together at the Rialto Ballroom on Upper Parliament Street, Queen's Hall in Widnes and two nights at the Tower Ballroom in New Brighton. The first night at the Tower Ballroom was 21 September and was oddly advertised as 'Rory Storm's Birthday Night'. His birthday was in fact in January, but it is clear that promoter Sam Leach was giving the group a much needed boost after the loss of Ringo. On the bill with The Hurricanes and Beatles were The Big Three, Billy Kramer and The Coasters and Buddy Dean and The Teachers. October 12 saw both bands back at the Tower Ballroom for 'Operation Big Beat 6' alongside The Undertakers, The Remo Four featuring Johnny Sandon, Billy Kramer and The Coasters, The Four Jays, The Merseybeats, The Big Three, Pete Maclaine and The Dakotas, and Lee Curtis and The All Stars, who featured Pete Best on drums. An awkward silence took place when Pete walked past The Beatles backstage. The 1 legend Little Richard was booked to top the bill for a great night of entertainment. The Beatles had released their first single 'Love Me Do' the previous week.

The Litherland Town Hall, The Cassanova Club, Orrel Park Ballroom and The Iron Door all bore host to The Hurricanes in the coming weeks. They could still pull the crowds and entertain. Johnny told Rory that they needed to learn new numbers to play as their set was going stale, but Rory was not so keen on the idea. Other bands were flying past them in the pecking order as they strove for ever-changing sets. The competition was fierce, and Johnny knew it. Rory remained convinced that a show was what people needed to see, and he became much more wilder than before. At the New Brighton Pier he climbed onto the glass roof of the pavilion and started to dance, before it gave way and he fell through before landing on the stage. He was cut and bleeding, but that was no excuse for him to stop the show, so on he went.

New Brighton Pier where Rory fell through the glass roof. (Photographer unattributed. Courtesy and permission from the collection at Wallasey Central Reference Library)

The Hurricanes playing at the New Brighton Pavilion. The photo has clearly been printed in reverse as the lads are all playing left-handed. (Courtesy of Iris Caldwell)

On 15 December, the Mersey Beat Poll Winner's Concert took place at the Majestic Ballroom in Birkenhead, with The Hurricanes being invited to take part. The Beatles were announced as the winners, with The Hurricanes now slipping down to nineteenth place. It was a huge fall from grace for the band who were not so long ago the biggest thing in Merseyside, though, again, they had spent a lot of time outside of Merseyside. The lads carried on with the hope that their chance would come. They may have been slipping in the ranks and not changing along with the other Merseyside groups, but when it came to putting on a show they were still number one.

Rory and Ringo had been good for one another. Rory had pushed Ringo to do things that he may never otherwise have done – changing his name and singing in his own slot during shows. Ringo had been a calming influence on Rory, making him feel good with his silly humour. In the three years that Ringo played with the band it was noticeable that Rory's stammer had improved vastly. After he left them, the stutter began to hound Rory once more, though he still refused to allow it to stop him doing anything.

6

Runaway Drummers

The Hurricanes started the year with a few bookings, including at the Iron Door where they were now playing on a regular basis. They liked it there and went down well with the punters. They also returned to one of their old haunts at the Majestic Ballroom in Crewe. Gibson Kemp left the band in early 1963 to join Kingsize Taylor and The Dominoes in Germany. Gibson later formed the group 'Paddy, Klaus & Gibson', with Paddy Chambers and Klaus Voormann, who were signed by Brian Epstein. In 1967 he married Astrid Kirchherr and had a glittering career working in the record industry. In 1974 he married for a second time, to Christina Werner. The couple have run a successful pub/restaurant called 'Kemps Bar' in Hamburg for a number of years. Gibson still plays with his band 'London Pride' and performed with The Dominoes during their farewell concert in August 2015. The Hurricanes were now without a drummer once more, and so began a period of them struggling to keep hold of one. Rory was later to comment: 'We train them, then other bands take them.'

They had six gigs booked over three days at the start of February. A guy called Deni sat in with them to help them out at The Orrell Park Ballroom. Knotty Ash village Hall, Hollyoake Club, Iron Door and the Majestic Ballroom in Crewe. Brian Johnson joined them on drums as they set about playing at many of their familiar venues – the Cavern, Tower Ballroom, and of course the Jive Hive. They also appeared at the Peppermint Lounge on London Road, which had previously been called the Cassanova Club. Out of town they played again at the Majestic Ballroom in Crewe, Civic Hall in Ellesmere Port, and the Queens Hall, Widnes.

The Inland Revenue contacted the group regarding a rather large tax bill. When Ringo had joined The Beatles, Brian Epstein had wanted everything above board. Ringo had to declare how long he had played with The Hurricanes so that his tax could be paid. Unfortunately the rest

No. 54 Broad Green Road. Rory alongside Barbara Denton. She and her sister would clean his car whenever he was returning from Hamburg, Butlins etc. (Courtesy of Iris Caldwell)

of the band now received the same bill, £13,000 each. They were stunned and booked an appointment with the solicitor Rex Makin to see what they could do. In the end expenses were worked out and the bill was reduced to an affordable amount. Walter Eymond has put to bed another false story that appears in many Beatle books: Ringo did not pay the band's tax bill; it was Rex Makin who helped them deal with it.

On 8 May the band attended a recording session at the Rialto Ballroom on Upper Parliament Street. Oriole Records had come up to Liverpool following the success of a number of the area's groups and singers. They wanted to record two albums under the title 'This Is Mersey Beat', which would include a number of local groups that had not yet made any chart success. The Hurricanes performed 'Dr Feel Good', 'I Can Tell' and 'Talkin About You', with Rory singing, before Lu took over the vocals for their version of 'Beautiful Dreamer'. When you consider that they were recorded on a landing at the top of a stairwell in the Rialto for extra acoustics, you have to agree that the songs turned out pretty darn good. Not long after the recordings Brian Johnson was off, joining Mark Peters and The Silhouettes, and they found themselves without a drummer once more. The two volumes of the album were released a few weeks later on 5 July. 'Talkin About You' did not feature by them; instead a version of the song by Faron's Flamingos made it onto the LP. The Hurricanes' recording of 'Talkin About You' has never surfaced.

Keith 'Keef' Hartley from the Thunder Beats was the next drummer to join The Hurricanes. He played with them at a number of dates around the local area, before they were asked to perform at The Cavern on 18 June for a television documentary called *Beat City*. In the show they were filmed singing 'I Can Tell', dressed in smart black suits and moving from side to side. Cavern regular Pat Davies talked on camera about Rory, telling how he once threw toast at someone because it had jam on it, and of the night that he told Pat he would give her a lift home, with Pat thinking how kind he was until he dropped her off at a cemetery.

Johnny's brother and Pat married at St George's Hall, and the band members were all in attendance. Pat spoke of what they did to him that day for a joke: 'They bought about a ton of scrap metal and tied it to my car. There was so much of it that they had to hide it underneath. As I drove away towards the Mersey Tunnel I heard a terrible screeching sound and I thought the bottom of the car had fallen out. Then, the police came running towards me to stop me going into the tunnel. They saw the funny side of it and helped cut the scrap free and sent us on our way to our honeymoon.'

When the 'This is Mersey Beat' albums were released on 5 July, the band were on their way to Middlesbrough for a gig at the Astoria Ballroom. The following day they bought their copies and were very pleased with them. It was not huge fame, but hey, they were on an album! The local gigs continued, along with the trips to play at the Majestic in Crewe. On 31 July they played an audition at the Orrell Park Ballroom for a forthcoming contract in Hamburg, Germany. They passed, and were given a start date for October. Then came the August bank holiday on Monday 5, and another much talked about Rory Storm moment.

A 'Beat and Bathe Show' had been arranged at the outdoor swimming pool in New Brighton. A number of bands had been booked to play as the public swam, or chilled in the evening sun while listening to the music. Over 1,500 people had turned up, and Rory was about to treat them to

The highest diving board at New Brighton outdoor pool which Rory dived from. (Photographer unattributed. Courtesy and permission from the collection at Wallasey Central Reference Library)

something special. The Hurricanes were announced and performed a few numbers before bursting into 'What'd I Say'. Rory belted it out up to the lead guitar break, then climbed the steps up to the top diving board. The band played on and Rory stripped off his clothes to reveal a tiny pair of gold swimming trunks. He walked to the end of the diving board, bounced, dived into a somersault and landed perfectly in the water. Coming back up, he swam to the edge, climbed out of the pool, picked up the microphone and carried on with the song. The crowd went crazy, the applause rang out and everyone looked on in admiration at the crazy singer. Nobody, but nobody, did it like Rory.

The following week they took part in the filming of the documentary *The Mersey Sound* at The Cavern club. The TV companies were swarming to Liverpool after the rise to fame of The Beatles and other local groups and singers. This was all good news for bands like The Hurricanes, who were given exposure and a TV appearance.

In October 1963, The Hurricanes flew to Hamburg for their booking at the Star-Club where they were to play a rotation system of two sets each alongside Kingsize Taylor and the Dominoes and Freddie Starr and the Midnighters. They appeared at the Star-Club from 10 October to 10 November. While there they also played on the bill with Duane

1. No. 54 Broad Green Road. Family home of the Caldwells. Alan's bedroom was top right.

2. The Gardeners Arms public house was very close to the Caldwell home and was used by the family for social events. Vi and Winnie Mac would go here on a Sunday evening. The building was demolished a few years ago.

3. St Vincent's hospice, Broad Green Road. Ernest Caldwell would give his time to help out here.

4. Old Swan Youth Club on Derby Lane with Martin's Dance Centre next door. Rory, Johnny, Ty and Lou were all members of both centres.

5. The bathroom, top left, at No. 54 Broad Green Road. It is from here that Alan heard someone playing guitar, discovering later that it was John Byrne.

6. The garden at No. 54 Broad Green Road where Ernie built the Anderson shelter during the Second World War. The roof you see over the fence is the roof of John Byrne's house in Oakhill Park.

7. The stairway of No. 54 Broad Green Road (the wood was brown back in the 1950s). Ritchie would play his drums by the cupboard, while the rest of the lads would sit on the stairs playing guitars.

8. No. 37 Oakhill Park, home of John Byrne.

9. The original front door and tiled step at John Byrne's house.

10. All that remains of Balgownie are the stone gateposts. They are a huge part of the Merseybeat history.

11. Balgownie name on the gatepost.

12. No. 49 Pemberton Road, home of Charles O'Brien.

13. No. 9 Madryn Street, birthplace of Richard Starkey. (Courtesy of Ged Fagan)

14. No. 10 Admiral Grove, home of Richard Starkey. (Courtesy of Ged Fagan)

15. No. 11 Ulster Road, Old Swan, home of the Eymond family after they were bombed out during the Second World War.

16. No. 20B The Green. The top-floor flat on the left is the family home of Walter Eymond.

17. Lowlands in West Derby. The Hurricanes played here a number of times.

18. The Rory Storm trophy, awarded to the winner of the 3000-metre steeplechase. (Courtesy of The Liverpool and Pembroke Harriers Athletics Club)

19. West Derby Stocks. Johnny sat in these for a laugh and was nearly caught by a policeman.

20. The guys wearing their new suits for Butlins. (Courtesy of Iris Caldwell)

21. The Indra club where The Beatles were playing when The Hurricanes arrived in Hamburg.

22. The Kaiserkeller club. It was here that The Hurricanes first played in Hamburg, and were shortly to be joined at the club by The Beatles.

23. Inside the Kaiserkeller. A lot has changed since 1960, but the atmosphere of this historic club still remains, as does a small part of the old stage.

24. No. 10 Oakhill Park, home of Iris and Shane after their marriage.

25. The Top Ten Club.

26. The Hamburg police station where Rory was taken. Also, the station where Pete Best and Paul McCartney were held after lighting a condom at the Bambi Kino and being accused of arson. George Harrison was held here after being found to be under the age of eighteen.

27. The old Studio X club, located above The Kaiserkeller. Rory played here a number of times after being sacked by Bruno.

28. This shop was the former leather store where Rory, Johnny, and The Beatles bought their jackets. It is located on the Reeperbahn, opposite the Grosse Freiheit.

29. Gretel & Alfons pub, Grosse Freiheit, Hamburg. The Lads from The Hurricanes would often drink here. It is located just yards away from the Star-Club and Kaiserkeller.

30. Hotel Pacific and room 403. The Hurricanes stayed here in 1963 when they were booked for the Star-Club. Rory, Johnny and Keith Hartley shared room 403.

31. The Knotty Ash Hall, scene of many gigs for the band.

32. The Hurricanes at the Orrell Park Ballroom. (Courtesy of Walter Eymond)

33. Jimmy Tushingham on drums while Lou sings. The lady in front of Ty is his girlfriend Irene, while the lady with her back to the camera is Lou's girlfriend Yoelande. (Courtesy of Walter Eymond)

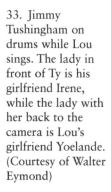

Left: 34. A 1964 poster for a Merseybeat charity football match. (Courtesy of Iris Caldwell)

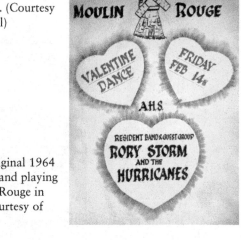

Right: 35. Original 1964 poster of the band playing at the Moulin Rouge in Liverpool. (Courtesy of Iris Caldwell)

Left: 36. 1987 poster for the play *The Need for Heroes*.(Courtesy of Eddie Porter)

Right: 37. 1992 poster for the play *Beautiful Dreamer*.(Courtesy of Eddie Porter)

38. 1992 poster for *Rorytania*. (Courtesy of Eddie Porter)

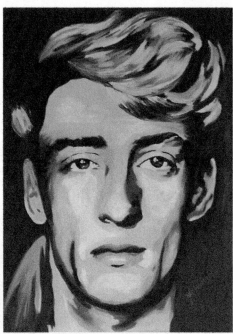

Above left: 39. An original poster from a 1963 gig in Millom, Cumbria. (Courtesy of Iris Caldwell)

Above right: 40. This painting of Rory was presented to Iris by a young female artist. Today it hangs proudly on the wall of her home.

Right: 41. Iris Caldwell next to the painting of her brother at Johnny Guitar's house. This portrait was painted by the same lady who presented Iris with her painting of Rory. (Courtesy of Iris Caldwell)

42. Walter Eymond.

43. Gaz Wato's wonderful drawing of Rory Storm. (Courtesy of Gaz Wato)

44. Rory's sister Iris with Johnny Guitar and his wife Margaret. Iris is holding Johnny's Antoria guitar. (Courtesy of Iris Caldwell)

45. The Simon Pritchard Painting of The Hurricanes playing at New Brighton Tower Ballroom. (Courtesy of Simon Pritchard)

46. The Hurricanes cast posing before the play *The King Of Liverpool*. (Courtesy of Carl Wharton)

47. The trophy presented to Rory after he broke the Harriers 3-mile record. The author of this book returned the shine to the trophy with the help of a little brasso.

48. Rory playing golf. (Courtesy of Iris Caldwell)

49. Rory checking the look. (Courtesy of Iris Caldwell)

Looking towards the Star-Club on the left of photograph. (Courtesy of Ted Kingsize Taylor)

Eddy (1–3 November), The Three Bells, Bobby Patrick Big Six, and Tony Sheridan. A Star-Club receipt signed by Rory Storm shows the club paying the bands flight expenses from the UK to Germany.

On arrival in Hamburg, Johnny, Rory, and Keith Hartley checked into the Hotel Pacific on the Neuer Pferdemark, a mere five-minute walk from the Star-Club. The three of them shared room No. 403. The Star-Club would use this hotel for most of their bands and would pay the hotel expenses for them. The hotel receipt shows that Rory booked in as Alan Caldwell, clearly the name on his passport; he still signed the bill Rory Storm. This is one of many documents to prove that he did not, as is stated so often, change his name by deed poll. Lou and Ty shared another room at the hotel. It was a far better place than any that they had stayed at during their time in Hamburg in 1960, and it offered them easy access to the Grosse Freiheit and the Star-Club.

Sadly ignorance was to rear its ugly head during their stint at the Star-Club, with many of the punters thinking that Rory's stammer was hilarious. They would take advantage of it by requesting him to do numbers such as 'Do you Love Me', which Rory always had difficulty with due to the speaking part in the intro. People can be very cruel, but

Left: The Hotel Pacific bill for Johnny, Rory and Keith Hartley, who were all staying in room 403. (Courtesy of the Thorsten Knublauch collection)

Below: Hotel Pacific receipt signed by Rory Storm. (Courtesy of the Thorsten Knublauch collection)

Lou Walters in Gretel & Alfons pub, 1963, pictured with barmaid Rita. (Courtesy of Ted Kingsize Taylor)

praise to Rory for seeing it through even though it must have hurt him, a far braver thing than sitting within a group of ignorant people who mock.

In November, while still in Germany, The Hurricanes and The Midnighters swapped drummers; Keef Hartley left Rory and the boys, and Ian Broad was welcomed by them. Once more the curse of the drummer had struck them, and it was to raise its head again very quickly when, after arriving back in the UK, Ian Broad left to join The Seniors. Trevor Morais came to them from the Flamingos, but the question was, how long for?

While in Hamburg The Hurricanes would frequent many of the bars that were popular with the Merseyside bands, including Gretal and Alfons, The Beer Shop and The Flunder Bar. The bands also ate at the Chung-ou Chinese restaurant and the cafe moller. There was a great camaraderie between the bands who knew each other from back home in Liverpool. They were young and life was good. Lou used his rifle skills to win a giant white teddy bear at the local fairground (The Dom). It was over 4 feet tall and he carried it all the way back to Liverpool to give to his girlfriend Yoelande.

The lads in the band had to go to the main police station in Hamburg to get their passports checked and stamped so that they could work. On arrival, Rory saw the queues, decided he was not waiting and walked to

One of the rarest photographs to be found. Rory Storm and The Hurricanes performing at the Star-Club, Hamburg, in 1963. (Courtesy of Iris Caldwell)

the front. An officer shouted at him in German and motioned him to join the back of the line, but Rory refused and said, 'I thought we got rid of you lot in 1945.' Lou told Rory to behave and get in line, but Rory was now on a roll and kept shouting insults. They reached the front before being told to go up to another level. The building had walk-in lifts with no doors; you just stepped in and back out at your floor. As the guys walked into the lift Rory aimed another comment towards the officer and Lou flipped. Grabbing Rory by the throat, he called him a stupid idiot. As he did Ty's face appeared over Lou's shoulder and he said, 'You better pull him back in as the ceiling is coming.' When grabbing hold of Rory, Lou had pushed him out through the open door and was dangling him in the air as the lift moved up. Quickly he pulled him back inside before they had a squashed Rory.

One day during their time in Hamburg Lou was approached by Paul Rogers who had played with The Texans and recorded the songs with Johnny guitar at the Percy Phillips studio in Kensington, Liverpool. Paul was now working for Polydor in Germany, and asked Lou along to a meeting about possible song recordings. Lou was invited for a meal, then taken to the Polydor studio that held the demo tapes. Here he was asked to listen to a few demos and pick out a few that he liked. He did this

Lou Walters portrait taken upstairs at the Star-Club, Hamburg. (Courtesy of Walter Eymond)

before being asked if he would like to record them. Then the bombshell was dropped. The offer only applied to him, not The Hurricanes. Lou told them 'You take us as we are or not at all', and walked out of the office. After returning to Liverpool, Polydor would still write to Lou and ask him to leave the band. The fact that he never left shows just how strong the bond was between these guys.

The Mersey Sound documentary was broadcast in October 1963, with the *Beat City Show* being shown in December. Both programmes featured The Hurricanes; they were on the telly. When they had recorded the songs for the 'This Is Mersey Beat' albums back in May, they had also signed a royalty contract with Oriole Records. The company contacted them with

Rory Storm portrait taken upstairs at the Star-Club, Hamburg. (Courtesy of Iris Caldwell)

the information that they were releasing a single of The Hurricanes songs from the album. 'Dr Feel good' would be the A side and 'I Can Tell' the B. The lads were delighted; their own record. The single was released in December of 1963 and sold among their local fans, but never hit the charts. Maybe 'I Can Tell' would have been a better choice of A side? Really, the record label was not big enough to produce a hit.

'Dr Feelgood' had become a popular song for Rory to perform. It was early in 1962 when Ted 'Kingsize' Taylor introduced the song to him at the Plaza in St Helens. Rory asked Ted if he would write out the lyrics of the song for him. Ted agreed, and they went to the Chinese restaurant across the road. While they waited for their food, Ted wrote the words from the song onto a white serviette for Rory. It became a popular number on the Hurricanes set list.

Iris Caldwell had been dating Paul McCartney, though Brian Epstein had insisted that their romance was kept a secret as he did not want fans knowing they were dating, or, as in John's case, married. Paul was busy as The Beatles' careers took off, though they still met up from time to time. One night Paul and Ringo called at Iris's house after driving up from London where they had been recording. They were tired and Vi offered them something to eat as they sat around the table. Ringo said, 'As we drove through Old Swan we hit a dog.' Iris asked was the dog OK? They replied, 'No idea? We were too tired to stop.' Iris was horrified and Rory and Vi were angry. They had their own dog called Toby who they all adored. Vi told them to leave the house, telling them that they were heartless. They were of course joking, but Iris wanted nothing more to do with Paul. Plus she knew that Jane Asher was now on the scene.

On 15 December, at the Locarno Ballroom, The Hurricanes found out that they had been placed eighteenth in the Mersey Beat Poll. Just two years earlier they had won the poll before being demoted to fourth place. Now they were just getting into the top twenty – still very respectable, but not what had been expected from them. To be fair though, The Hurricanes had spent a lot of the year outside of Merseyside.

Rory could be a crazy performer and was always seeking to go further for the delight of the crowds. Perhaps his craziest, dangerous and most comical stunt took place on 10 January 1964, when the band played at the Majestic Ballroom in Birkenhead. Rory had contacted the local press to tell them that if they wanted a good photograph they should get themselves along to the Majestic as he was going to leap from a balcony onto the stage. True to his word, as The Hurricanes played Rory climbed up to the balcony, held on as he posed for any photos, slipped, fell, and landed at the side of the stage. Everyone looked on in horror, before he dragged himself to his feet and climbed back up on the stage. Rory was clearly in pain, but he refused to end the gig and carried on singing (well

Lou in the Beer-Shop next to the Star-Club, Hamburg 1963. (Courtesy of Ted Kingsize Taylor)

he was a real showman), before going home feeling unwell. Later that night his family called an ambulance and he was admitted to Broadgreen Hospital.

The newspaper report from the *Liverpool Echo*, dated 11 January 1964, reads, 'RORY STORM TAKEN TO CITY HOSPITAL'. It continued: 'Liverpool beat star Rory Storm, aged 24, was taken to Broadgreen hospital last night, a few hours after he fell 30ft from the balcony of the Majestic Ballroom, Birkenhead, where he was appearing with his group The Hurricanes. After the fall, Rory (real name Alan Caldwell), got to his feet and sang two more numbers, before going home. His mother, Mrs Violet Caldwell, said at her home in Broad Green Road, Liverpool, today, that Rory came home last night and went to bed feeling unwell. "He had severe pain in his chest during the night, so we called an ambulance. It's ironical that his latest record should be called 'Doctor Feel Good'", she added. Rory is being kept in hospital for observation. A hospital spokesman said this afternoon that he was fairly comfortable.'

Rory was admitted to Broad Green Hospital. From here he phoned the local press who sent a photographer to snap him with the nurses. He never missed an opportunity did Rory. A number of books report that Rory broke his leg in this fall when in fact he actually broke his ribs and badly sprained his ankle, so much so that it was put into plaster. He did break a leg on another occasion and an arm in a separate incident. Did the injury stop Rory performing? No! He was the ultimate showman. Limping onto a stage with a crutch under one arm, he would tell the audience, 'I will just leave this over here', as he put down the crutch and started to sing. He was admitted to hospital so many times that one local newspaper came up with the headline 'RORY BACK IN BROAD GREEN' after one of his mishaps. Just out of interest, Rory was allergic to penicillin.

Ted 'Kingsize' Taylor recalled the event when Rory broke his leg: 'The Dominoes were on the same bill as The Hurricanes for a gig at the Plaza in St Helens. We were watching their performance when Rory decided to climb up to the balcony where he proceeded to jump the 14-foot distance onto the stage. Of course being Rory he did it in style, holding a 2-foot pink comb in his hand as he descended. As he hit the stage his leg broke, although that was never going to stop his crowd pleasing. Lying on the stage he began combing his hair, as if nothing had happened. We all fell about laughing.'

Trevor Morais left the group to join The Peddlers. The curse of Ringo was hitting the band hard. The Beatles were by now big stars, and the questions to The Hurricanes would mostly be about their ex-drummer. Ringo this, Ringo that. It was becoming tiresome to the lads. No wonder drummers were not staying with them if they were being compared to Ringo by so many people.

The band struggled without a permanent drummer. Practice was almost impossible, and the band's playing skills fell with no regular beat-maker behind them. They still refused to move with the times. Rock 'n' Roll was their game, and while you can never question their loyalty to it, their set was not changing much, thus becoming a bit stale. But when it came to a show they were fantastic and would have the audience bouncing.

This photo taken at Gretal & Alfons bar in Hamburg, features two ex-Hurricanes. From left to right: Brian Johnson (Ex Drums-Hurricanes) Noddy (Brian) Redman, Billy J Kramer, Ted Kingsize Taylor, Bobby Thomson (ex-bass player for The Hurricanes). (Courtesy of Ted Kingsize Taylor)

Jimmy Tushingham now joined them on drums in February of 1964, with the ex-Four Clefs drummer informing them that he would play with them at least until the year was out. This was great news for the band, who were in much need of a regular drummer. Jimmy had heard from Jamo that the band were in search of a drummer and was told that they would be playing a charity football match against the fire brigade at the Jacobs sports field on Longmoor Lane in Aintree.

Jamo told Jimmy to come along to the football match and talk to the lads after the game, so he did. Watching from the touchline he saw a player get injured, before Rory and the lads asked him would he play. Wanting to impress them he said yes, even though he could hardly play. They asked him what position he played and he blurted out 'outside left'. The guys were impressed; they had never had an outside left player. So Jimmy changed, walked on and proceeded to get booted everywhere by the firemen. It was clear that he was no footballer. After the game when he was changing, Rory came over to talk to Jimmy: 'I believe you play the drums?' he asked him, before telling him that they had a gig at the Casino Ballroom in Accrington if he wanted to try out with them. Jimmy agreed and Rory said, 'You better be fucking better at drumming than you are at football.'

Jimmy had been born in Liverpool in late 1943. He made his debut in Accrington, where he watched Rory leap around the stage before jumping up onto a piano that had a cloth on top of it, sliding off, and falling to the floor. The lads asked him to join them, but told him he needed a better drum kit. Jimmy duly purchased a gold Trixon set of drums.

The gigs continued at the regular venues, with Jimmy fitting in well. By now, many of their old friends had found success in the charts – The Beatles, Cilla Black, Gerry and The Pacemakers, Billy J. Kramer and The Dakotas, The Searchers, and The Swinging Blue Jeans. Many others had signed recording deals and released a number of records. The Hurricanes had not given up hope that their day would come. Rory's house was still a hangout for bands late at night, and Vi was always ready to welcome them. As the cars pulled up in the early hours Vi would emerge and usher them all inside so as not to disturb the neighbours. One night as she was shushing and pushing them into the house Rory opened his bedroom window and started throwing footballs out into the street while Vi, worrying about the neighbours, ran down Broad Green Road picking them up.

Astrid Kirchherr, who they had known in Hamburg when she was Stuart Sutcliffe's girlfriend, had come to Liverpool to photograph a number of places within the city. While here, she took a photo that included over 200 local band members who were pictured holding up their instruments on the steps of St George's Hall. The guys were all present and said hello to Astrid, who placed them in the centre of the group of musicians for the photo. Rory was combing his hair as it was taken, ever the perfectionist. Afterwards, Astrid chatted with the lads about the old days in Hamburg and expressed her sorrow that they had not yet made it big in the music

The lads arriving in Spain with Rory giving the 'V For Victory' Sign. Jimmy Jenkins is behind them on the right. (Courtesy of Iris Caldwell)

charts. Rory thanked her for the photo that she had taken of him in Hamburg, telling her how special it was to him.

Beatlemania was spreading fast and had found its way to the Balearic Islands off the coast of Spain. The Hurricanes were booked by the well-known Liverpool undertaker Jimmy Jenkins to play in Mallorca and Ibiza, and the Spanish press caught onto the fact that they were the ex-bandmates of Ringo Starr. The members of the group had met up at 2.00 p.m. at the La Bussola cafe on Bold Street, before taking a train from Lime Street station to Manchester airport. Here, they boarded a propeller plane for their flight to Barcelona, taking off at 9.15 p.m. and arriving just after two thirty in the morning (with the time difference the flight took slightly over four hours). Jimmy Tushingham described the plane as a cardboard box that gave them a few jitters along the way.

As the plane landed the journalists were waiting, and Rory was ready for them. When the door to the aircraft opened, Rory popped out, put a cigar in his mouth and gave the Winston Churchill 'V For Victory' sign. The Spanish loved him and rushed for an interview. When asked why he was visiting Spain, Rory replied 'To find some cows, but I have not seen any yet.' They then asked if his hair was a Beatle haircut. 'No!' he replied. 'It is a work of art, I created it.' Another member of the band on leaving the plane was asked what was in his bag, and told the reporters that it was a spider that ate Beatles.

The lads were put up in the Oriente Hotel, where Johnny almost had them evicted. He had taken a whistle from somewhere and was sat in the bath of his room blowing it down the overflow pipeline. Other guests had complained about the noise at reception, and a search discovered the culprit was Johnny. The hotel manager was furious and wanted them out, but they managed to talk him round and behaved themselves. That same day, at 5.00 p.m., they appeared on the TV show *Discorama* before being interviewed on local Barcelona radio at 9.00 p.m. The radio show was conducted in a small room with coconut mats and a mike hanging from the ceiling, which everyone stood around. Questions were asked in Spanish, then the lads were asked in English and their replies were translated.

They then had a couple of days to themselves before they moved to Majorca, plus a free bar at the hotel, so they experimented with bacardi and coke. The bacardi took hold of Jimmy Tushingham and the lads took their drunk drummer to his room. Somehow he managed to find his way outside and sat on a bench full of ladies who were the local prostitutes. The lads spotted him, took him back inside and put him to bed. The next night as they walked past the ladies on the bench, the girls started laughing and calling out 'Bambino' to Jimmy.

The Hurricanes then flew to Majorca where they were met by open-top cars. Some members of the Majorcan press were a little worried about

The Hurricanes on stage in Spain. (Courtesy of Iris Caldwell)

having a Rock 'n' Roll band on their island and warned their readers about the shocking shows that they would produce. This would lead to the peace, tranquility, and sanity of the island falling into despair. They warned of how tables and chairs would be smashed during riots as the band played. It appeared that some pressmen were not big fans of the Brits and their rocking and rolling music.

Their first performance was set for 23 June at the Haima Club in Palma, where they had signed a contract to play, and the stage backed onto a cliff. The posters advertising them made for some eye-catching reading: 'IDOLS OF THE YOUTH OF TODAY' or 'THE MOST SCANDALOUS SENSATIONAL CURRENT MUSIC' to 'THE CREATORS OF MUSICAL RHYTHM, BORN IN THE CAVES OF LIVERPOOL'. Many people turned up to watch the English group – excited youngsters and intrigued adults – and they would not be disappointed as the band soon had the crowd rocking away.

They were booked for a show at the Tagomago Club in Valldemossa, again going down well with the audience who Rory thrilled as he hung from the pine trees around the stage. The club owner explained that he would have liked to have given them a longer contract, but that he was scared his customers would smash his furniture, or that Rory would break all the pine trees in the area. Other venues played were the Eva Maria Hotel in Palma and a club called El Rodeo. While on the island the band had adopted the Trini Lopez hit 'America' from a group that they saw performing it in Palma, and it proved to be a favourite with the islanders and holidaymakers.

The guys enjoying the Spanish water. Lou is still wearing sunglasses. (Courtesy of Iris Caldwell)

The Hurricanes pictured with British footballers including Ian St John, Ron Yeats and Frank McLintock in Spain. (Courtesy of Iris Caldwell)

The guys received invitations to a party at a millionaire's villa. Many Spanish celebrities were present, along with the Jazz musician Tubby Hayes and footballers Ian St John and Ronnie Yeats. The Hurricanes were given their own table at the party, where a swimming pool had been filled with baby sharks and a tightrope was stretched across its length – guests were informed that it was just for show. Waiters walked around pushing trolleys full of champagne that they handed out to guest whenever they wanted one. A huge cruise ship off the coast was connected to someone at the party and Rory asked if he could go out and have a look around it. He was told that he could, and while he waited for a boat to take him out to the ship he noticed a jet-ski, so of he went over the waves, climbed up to the ship, took the tour, climbed down and jet-skied back.

The lads enjoyed some food and drink before being supplied with huge balls of ice-cream each. Jimmy Tushingham picked his ball up and threw it at Lou Walters, hitting him smack in the face. Then Lou threw his back and a food fight broke out. Shocked guest looked on before silence fell over the room and everyone looked towards the swimming pool. There, barefooted and walking the rope above the baby sharks, was Rory. Of course he fell in, causing many of those present to panic about his safety, but he was fine and climbed out of the pool.

Rory and the boys lived a charmed life, and it continued one night in a club in Palma. The band were up on stage when hundreds of sailors entered the club. They were serving on the JFK Aircraft Carrier that had docked in Palma, and they were looking for fun on their shore leave.

Hurricanes posing for a photograph on the rocks in Spain. (Courtesy of Iris Caldwell)

The club was jam-packed and the Americans were loving the Hurricanes' music, dancing on the tables and singing along. It was a great atmosphere, and then a fight broke out. The chairs and tables flew through the air as a mass brawl took hold. The band had to take cover before the MPs arrived in their jeeps and restored order. The lads later took up an invitation of a tour of the JFK Aircraft Carrier, being shown around before eating a meal of steak and chips onboard.

A few locals had complained about the noise during the evenings; shows would have to be cancelled if they did not turn their thumping music down. A toned-down version of The Hurricanes was unthinkable, but that is what happened for the remainder of their time in Palma. The promoters began to send the boys over to Ibiza to play at the bullrings where the noise would not bother anyone. The band often played on the same bill as the duo Nina and Frederick, with The Hurricanes entertaining the crowds with their rocking show. For one gig the lads all wore matador outfits as they performed. This was filmed on a cine camera, and a number of people from Liverpool have told of how they had watched the recording at Rory's house on Broad Green Road. It appears the film has been lost over the years; we can live in hope that it is discovered one day.

The band had been booked to play a private gig on one of the islands and were due to fly over on a small aircraft. Back then if you flew between the islands you did not book a ticket, you just turned up, paid your fare and stood in line. When the plane arrived the lads went through the gate to board, all, that is, apart from Jimmy, who had the gate closed on him as the plane was full. Jimmy would have to wait for the next flight over, and feeling a bit fed-up he stood first in the queue. Rory then appeared at the plane door and shouted to him to hurry up as there was a seat. Jimmy jumped over the fence and darted across the tarmac towards the plane. However, the police were in pursuit and caught Jimmy. He was sat on a chair next to the plane with the police around him asking questions. Looking up he saw Rory, who had his nose on the window mouthing the words 'sorry Jimmy, someone had gone for a piss'. Jimmy was allowed to fly over on another flight when he explained what had happened to the police. Of course, the lads all had a good laugh about it.

At one bullring Rory asked a worker where they kept the bulls and the guy beckoned him and the lads to follow. They arrived at a gate and went inside a large paddock area that had another gate around 30 feet away at its other side. The lads noticed that the worker was up above them on a walkway, then they saw the far gate open and a bull come through it. A mad scramble was made for the gate they had entered through by four of the lads. Rory had already climbed up the wall to safety. Once through, the gate was closed and they all went up on the walkway to see a baby bull staring back up at them.

Another great photo showing the guys having fun in the sea. (Courtesy of Iris Caldwell)

The Hurricanes had gone down well in Spain, with a number of TV and radio appearances giving them a short taste of stardom. They now faced the long journey home – a boat from Palma to Barcelona before a long train ride from there to Paris, then from Paris to Calais where they caught the ferry to Dover, before the train journey back to Liverpool. Johnny was probably sick on all the boats. Lou had purchased a back-up generator as the Spanish electricity tended to go down. His bass would be thumping away then fade to almost nothing. The generator fixed the problem, but it was very heavy and he had to carry it all the way back to Liverpool. Lou still has the generator today.

They returned to Liverpool for the event of the year – the wedding of Rory's sister Iris. On 31 August 1964, Iris Caldwell married Shane Fenton at All Saints Church on Broad Green Road, Liverpool. Iris was a natural beauty who looked great all of the time, but in a wedding dress she was absolutely stunning. Shane, Rory, Ty and Johnny donned top hats and tails with blue carnation flowers for the buttonholes costing one guinea each.

The night before the wedding, Violet Caldwell, with others, had dressed the church, having borrowed Ferns to decorate the charge for the church grounds at night. Earlier that same day Iris was in her house when a delivery was made. She shouted to Rory, 'Is it the wedding flowers?' He replied, 'Yes, and three cabbages.' Iris ran into the hall

This fantastic picture of the boys in Spain is Rory's sister Iris's favourite photograph of the band. She keeps it on display in her living room.

in panic and saw what Rory was going on about: the posies for the bridesmaids really did look like cabbages. 'That's it, I am not getting married,' she screamed. The wedding did go ahead, and Iris recalled how as she walked down the aisle she glanced back to see three bridesmaids each holding a cabbage.

Photos of the couple outside the church show Rory and Johnny holding up guitars above the bride and groom, while the bridesmaids held up dancing shoes on lace lines. White doves were released, and of course the press were in attendance with their cameras. Shane Fenton's real name was Bernard William Jewry and he had been born in Muswell Hill, London. He later went on to find fame as Alvin stardust. The couple moved into a house at No. 10 Oakhill Park just off Broad Green Road. Rory now moved out of the box bedroom into the much larger back one that Iris had vacated at their family home.

On the eve of the wedding the band had played a gig in Middlesbrough before driving back to No. 54 Broad Green Road, their intention being to drop off the gear and head into the city centre to their regular hangout at the Odd Spot Club on Bold Street. As the lads unloaded their instruments Rory opened the bedroom window and whispered 'shall we wear these to the club lads?' before throwing down the wedding suits for the following day. A short time later, the guys from the band all walked proudly into the Odd Spot wearing top hats and tails.

One time at the Odd Spot Club the bouncers had paid back Rory for a joke he had played on them. They pelted him with tomatoes before pulling him into a car, driving to the Pier Head and throwing him into the river. Thankfully he was a great swimmer, as the Mersey has a very strong current, but the bouncers did hang around to make sure that he got out. Another occasion at the club saw Freddie Starr trying to take on Rory in a silliness contest, only to find that Rory was not one to back down. Freddie, facing Rory, ripped a button off his shirt – Rory ripped one back. Freddie pulled his pants down and stood in his underwear, as did Rory, and on it went, ending with them throwing buckets of water over one another.

Not long after the wedding Rory went into the Blue Angel club on Seel Street. Brian Epstein was in there and Rory went over to ask him why he

The wedding of Iris and Shane. Rory is between his sister and his mum and dad. Spot Johnny far right. (Courtesy of Iris Caldwell)

had not given The Hurricanes a helping hand after pinching Ringo. After chatting for a few minutes, Brian told Rory that he would help them make a record and that he would pay for it and produce it, but it was not a recording contract. He also told Rory to keep quiet about it or he would have to cancel the recording. Rory was ecstatic, and raced off to tell the other band members. With Brian Epstein helping them they felt certain that this was their chance of hitting the big time.

A letter came through the door of No. 54 Broad Green Road on 26 September 1964. It was postmarked in London and stamped 'Confidential'. It was from Brian Epstein, inviting the band to a recording session in London on 30 September. Again, Brian informed Rory not to tell anybody or the deal was off. Rory of course could keep nothing in and informed everyone he saw, even reporters from the local press. The session was not cancelled and the group, along with Iris and her husband Shane Fenton, travelled down to London on the morning of the 30th. They arrived at the studios on time and were shown inside, before Brian came in and asked them to play the songs that they thought he should consider using. They played most of their repertoire, but Brian was unimpressed, saying no to all of them. They then played 'America', the song that had thrilled the locals in Mallorca and Ibiza. Brian was happy; this was the song.

They all got to work on recording the song, which took a few hours to complete. Ringo, who had come to bring the lads cigarettes and to see

A check of the hair and all looks fine. (Courtesy of Iris Caldwell)

how they were getting on, sang along on backing vocals with Brian, Iris and Shane. At one point they retired to a nearby cafe to write a few new lines for the song. When the song was complete the engineer asked Lou to sing the final note again – over and over he kept saying 'do it again higher'. Everyone else had left by now and Lou was getting rather fed up with this guy asking for more. After giving a high note, Lou looked him in the eye and told him that was it, he had finished. The guy saw Lou's anger and replied, 'That is fine, we have it.' The song chosen for the B side was 'Since You Broke My Heart', sung by Lou. Brian told the band he would let them know when the single was due to be released. They then made their way back to Liverpool, unsure of how wise it was of Brian to choose that song, but hey, he knew his job!

Brian had also sent the band to visit an agent in London to tie up royalty rights and TV bookings for the single, and they found themselves sitting in the waiting room with The Kinks. The Hurricanes had played a gig in Mold, North Wales, the week before the recording, where their fee was £45. The agent asked to see their next few bookings as he was going to cover them for the next few weeks. One included a return to the club in Mold and the agent mistakenly wrote the fee down as £450 and invoiced the club. The lads were rather happy when they received their fee, but the club owner never booked them again.

Lou Walters on his wedding day with his bride Yoelande Madeira. Ty Brien (far left), Lou, Yoelande, Jimmy Tushingham, and Johnny Guitar. (Courtesy of Walter Eymond)

Back in their hometown the shows continued. Lou married his fiancée Yeolande Irene Madeira on 5 October at the Blessed Sacrament church on Walton Vale. Ty was his best man and all the lads from the band attended, while Ringo, along with fellow Beatles Paul and George, managed to make it to the ceremony without being detected by the media. Yoelande had been born on 11 March 1944 in Calcutta, India. She arrived in London on 16 July 1957 aboard the P&O passenger ship *Strathmore* before her family settled at No. 9 Lee Road in Knowsley. Yoelande had been working as a student nurse when she met Lou, later progressing to a full-time nurse.

Ty and his girlfriend Irene took Jimmy Tushingham to the Tudor Rooms in Southport to celebrate his twenty-first birthday, and bought him an expensive white shirt. The band still hoped for fame, and maybe the coming single would give them their opportunity. Johnny though, was unconvinced, and kept telling the others 'it is the wrong song', while Rory remained upbeat and hopeful. They received news that the single would be released just before Christmas.

On 11 December they filmed 'America' for the popular children's TV show *The Five O'Clock Club*. It was broadcast four days later, the same night that they appeared at The Cavern with The Chants, a much underrated Liverpool group. If you are wondering why they were on a children's TV show, let me explain. *The Five O'Clock Club* was hugely popular, with many top acts appearing on the show. They had been given a prime-time slot on TV. Unfortunately for them the song sucked big time, and while they had done a good job of recording it, it was never going to make a dent in the charts.

Sadly, Johnny was proven correct when the single flopped. He knew it was the wrong song; the guys probably knew it, and you have to wonder if Brian Epstein had known it as well? Their fans bought it, but it never got close to the charts. To be brutally honest, it was a hopeless song choice that never stood a chance of being a hit. It was possibly the worst song that they performed during their sets, and while it had gone down well with the locals and holidaymakers in the Balearics, it was useless as a single. It was what it was – a holiday song – and you have to wonder just why Brian had chosen it. Was he just a hopeless producer? Was he no good at recognising a hit song? Or did he know that the song was no good?

Many things have been said and written about Brian Epstein and The Hurricanes, but would he have intentionally tried to finish off their career with this record? It is impossible to say, but a number of people believe he was worried about the band, in particular Rory. Tall, good looking, built like an athlete, looking like a movie star. Was Rory too much a threat in Brian's eyes towards The Beatles? They were totally different types of bands, and there was room for them both? But again, this is all just pure speculation ...

Lou on his wedding day with his best man, Ty. (Courtesy of Walter Eymond)

The band recorded two songs at the Abbey Road studio in London in late 1964, 'Ubangi Stomp' and 'I'll Be There', though neither was ever released. It is claimed that Ringo offered to pay for a recording studio if the band wanted one to use, but for some reason they never took him up on his offer. Both Walter Eymond and Jimmy Tushingham have no recollection of this offer ever having been made. An eventful year came to a close. The touring, recording, TV appearances and Lou's wedding had made it an exciting ride. What would 1965 bring?

7

The Beginning of the End

The year 1965 started with a gig at the Technical College in Birkenhead. With them on the bill were Vince Earl and The Talismen and The Tagg. They also took part in a recording for a Radio Luxembourg show on 24 January at The Cavern, alongside Victor Bronx Blues Train and Kris Ryan and The Questions. The Hurricanes continued to stay loyal to Rock 'n' Roll, still playing a lot of the numbers that they had done several years earlier. Bands had sprung up everywhere, with the competition for work becoming fierce. While bookings had gone down, the band still had plenty of work. They could still pull a crowd and put on a great show, and Rory was still as crazy as ever up front. Johnny, Lou and Ty again suggested they should learn some new numbers and mix their set up a bit. Rory was not really interested; he was happy being a Rock 'n' Roll star.

The group were offered a contract in Germany. Good money and work abroad was always welcomed by the boys, but they had a problem – Lou was unhappy. Johnny and Lou had started to write their own songs and had put it to Rory that they wanted to try a few on stage. They explained to him that the group needed to expand its set, but Rory was happy ruling Merseyside. The guys knew their chance was still there if they changed a few things. Lou became disheartened by Rory's refusal to adapt to change and left the band. The lads wished him well, but it hurt them deeply; they were all like brothers. With the German tour approaching they needed a new bass player. Vince Earl, the frontman with the Talismen, agreed to join them and play bass.

The German tour date is uncertain, but Jimmy Tushingham remembered that it was very cold, so probably early '65. The band travelled by train to Germany, taking twenty-four hours to get there, arriving at the Storyville Club in Frankfurt just before 3.00 p.m. The club was on the second floor and was reached by climbing a big steel outside staircase. Crowds of people had already started lining the staircase, so the lads had to push past with their instruments. Once inside, John Stroader, who owned the club, told them they were due on stage in thirty minutes – so no time for a rest. As the band were getting ready to go on, Johnny appeared wearing leopard skin pants and shirt saying 'we are gonna wow them', much to the amusement of the others. They stayed at this club for a month, playing sets up to two in the morning and sharing the bill with the likes of Mal Ryder and The Spirits and The Beau Brummells. Next they moved on to Dusseldorf for two weeks. While here they spent a night drinking a Vat 69 whisky with Brian Casser, formerly of Cass and the Cassanovas. Brian was now in the band Casey Jones and The Engineers and their single had just reached number one in Germany. Their third and final stop on the tour was in Cologne. Here they played alongside a band called Dean Ford and The Gaylords, who went on to have a number of chart hits under their new name of Marmalade.

Pete Vernon's mother had known Rory's mum Vi from their dancing days together. One day they both bumped into each other at the shops in Old Swan. They chatted and Mrs Vernon mentioned that her son would go and watch Liverpool FC on his own by bus. Vi told her that Rory went to the games and would be happy to give Pete a lift. It was arranged, and Rory and Pete became good friends.

Rory was a sportsman, excelling in all events including football. At one time he had been on the books of the non-league side Prescot Cables, and had played with Liverpool FC reserves. Rory had set up a football team with Dave 'Jamo' Jamieson in 1959 at the youth club in Kirkby. Later it became called The Merseybeat Show Biz Eleven, featuring a

Still sitting on a wall at No. 54 Broad Green Road. This is where Rory wrote his name into wet cement so many years ago. It is so wonderful that it has survived.

number of local band members and some guest players. The team would play charity matches in the local area, taking on the likes of The Cavern Kickers, Crawfords Biscuits and other local teams. After each game, Rory and Jamo would collect donations from players and the people watching, before taking the money along to Alder Hey Children's Hospital. Ty, Lou and Johnny all played at times for the team, along with Freddie Starr, Vince Earl, Mike Gregory, Shane Fenton, Lee Baron, Eddie Amoo, Billy Kinsley, Freddie Marsden, Joey Bowers, Sam Leach, Pete Vernon, ex-Tranmere Rovers footballer Charlie McDonnell, who later ran the Vauxhall Vaults pub, and many more local guys. Tony Kay also joined them for games. Tony had been playing for Everton and had been widely tipped to be a part of England's 1966 World Cup squad. However, due to a bet he placed while playing for Sheffield Wednesday, he was harshly banned from the game for life. The author of this book was named after Tony Kay by his Everton-crazy father.

Rory even managed to get them a match against players from the first team squad of Liverpool FC at their Melwood training ground. He put his dad Ernie in goal for the game, with the musicians and footballers posing for a group photo afterwards. The photo was blown up and hung proudly on the wall at Rory's house in Broad Green Road. He also played five-a-side football with the Liverpool manager Bill Shankly. His swimming skills were put to use when he took a part-time job at Queens Drive swimming baths. Here he taught people to swim and how to dive. Rory had also started the Merseybeat Bowling league at the ABC bowling alley in Tue Brook. The league never lasted long due to lack of interest, or maybe because Rory was a great bowler who tended to win all the time.

Rory was a showman even when he played football, insisting on taking all the free kicks and penalties during a game. Of course this would mean stopping to pose for a photo before striking the ball. His father Ernie would be waiting on the sidelines to take the snap of his son in action and the celebration afterwards if he scored. Rory just had to have the limelight – he was the team captain – but to be fair to him he was a very good footballer, far above that of an average player. At one match the team was awarded a penalty kick. Up stepped Rory waving to his dad to get the camera ready. The ball was placed on the spot and Rory took a few steps backwards, took out his comb and fixed his hair for the pending photograph. As he did Sam Leach ran up and smacked the ball into the goal before running off, chased by a furious Rory.

Sam Leach would often play golf with Rory, and as Rory won all the time Sam started to wonder if he ever cheated. He did once catch Rory kicking his ball closer to the hole and made him move it right to the edge of the green. Rory then sunk a 30-foot putt to perfection, leaving Sam looking on in awe. On one occasion Rory even managed to get John

Lennon and Paul McCartney to join him and Sam for a round of golf at the Allerton course.

Wedding Bells were in the air again as Jimmy married Carol Byrnes in Bootle, soon to be followed by Ty, who married his sweetheart Irene Barlow on 19 June 1965 at St Oswald's church in Old Swan. They had been dance partners and had appeared on the TV show *Come Dancing*

Gate post to No. 54 Broad Green Road. You can spot where the small brass plaques used to sit on the posts with the word 'Stormsville'.

together. Irene was known to everyone as 'Barl' and had lived off Derby Lane in Old Swan. Another Hurricane would be married before the year was out. It was back to work for the boys, with engagements across the city as they kept the dream going. Vince Earl was not going to be part of that dream however, as he left the band in August of that year to join The Connoisseurs. Vince would go on to become a stand-up comedian, and would later play the part of Ron Dixon in the TV soap *Brookside*. Dave May was brought in on bass from Mark Peters and The Silhouettes.

On 1 August 1965, the phone rang at No. 54 Broad Green Road and Violet Caldwell answered it. After a quick conversation, she informed her husband Ernie, Iris and Rory that it had been Paul McCartney. He had told Violet to watch them on TV that evening on the show *Blackpool Night Out* as he was going to sing a song on his own and wanted her to listen to the words. After she had listened to it, he wanted her to decide if he was still the heartless guy that she had called him. The song that Paul sang was 'Yesterday'. They all watched him perform it, but we have no idea if Violet forgave him for the dog joke or for messing her daughter around.

Rumours are rumours, and it is hard to find the real truth on many of them. A number of rumours link Iris Caldwell to Beatle songs, after her being the one-time girlfriend of Paul McCartney. 'Yesterday' has been mentioned as being written about Iris, but would Paul really be writing about an old love who had since married? 'Love Me Do' is another, but this was written before Paul started seeing Iris. The rumour surrounding 'She Loves You' makes no sense as they had split up by then. The one rumour that could have some truth in it is that Paul wrote 'I Saw Her Standing There' about Iris. She was seventeen when he saw her dressed to kill, working as a dancer. 'Just Seventeen/They way she looked was way beyond compare/How could I dance with another', those words do sum up when Paul met Iris, so it is possible. Another rumour is that Paul wanted Rory Storm and The Hurricanes to sing 'I Saw Her Standing There', but Brian Epstein refused to let them. It would have fitted Rory well, but again we do not really know the truth on any of these rumours. Iris herself has informed the author that as far as she is concerned, Paul did not write any song about her; she would love it to be true, but it remains just a rumour. She also added that Paul told her he could not write a song about her as the only thing that rhymes with Iris is Virus.

Johnny married Eileen Manson in late 1965. The two, who had forever been splitting up, finally tied the knot. With both Ty and Johnny now married, touring abroad was no longer really an option. Johnny told Rory that maybe the band had now missed its chance of fame and that they could not go on forever. Rory was gutted; it had always been him and

The Hurricanes at the Tower Ballroom, New Brighton. (Courtesy of Walter Eymond)

Johnny from the start. They were getting older and settling down, and it was no surprise that secure, steady jobs had begun to appeal to the lads who wanted to start families. They would still be a band, but not as full on as it had been before.

Dave May left to join the band Phase Three in February 1966. Karl Terry joined the group on bass from The Cruisers. On 27 February, The Hurricanes played at The Cavern. The club was closing as it had gone bankrupt. Ray McFall told the bands that the bailiffs would be arriving the following morning to seize the club – this was the last farewell. The Big Three, The Dark Ages, The Hideaways, The Pro-Terms, Earl Preston's Realms, The Runaways, The Kwan, The Cryin Shames, The Sect, The Richmond Group, Rigg, and The Rekords joined Rory Storm and The Hurricanes on the final night. As Al Caldwell's Skiffle Group, Rory and Johnny had played The Cavern before any other beat group. They had been the star billing on the night that the club became a beat club, and here they were on the final night. They were as much a part of The Cavern club story as anybody, and they were not leaving without a fight. The bands barricaded the doorway – stuff the bailiffs. It gave everyone a good laugh, but they came to realise that it was all to no avail. The club was finished. Just after 5.00 a.m. on the morning of the 28th the bands began to leave The Cavern. The Cavern reopened in July of that year and hosted some great bands up to its forced closure in 1973, but it was never the beat club it had been in the early 1960s.

Rory with his Jag. (Courtesy of Iris Caldwell)

Iris and Shane had visited a market in Barcelona. While there they noticed a tiny baby monkey lying in a cage in its own excrement. It was clearly suffering, and Iris bought the poor creature with the intention of taking it to a vet to put it out of its misery. At the vets the monkey was given an injection and sprung into life. It was not going back to that market, so they brought it back to Liverpool. Here, it fell in love with Iris's dad Ernie. It followed him everywhere, and if he fell asleep in his chair it would creep up on him and pull the hairs from his nose. They called the monkey 'Guapa' ('beautiful' in Spanish). It may have loved Ernie, but Guapa was no fan of Vi. They had a plate rack above the kitchen sink and Guapa would hide there and throw plates at Vi when she came in. When Iris and her friends were getting ready to go out they had to be careful when putting on false eyelashes as Guapa liked to rip them off.

Rory would take Guapa out with him, a great pulling tool for the girls – not that he needed it. One night as he was driving home, Rory saw a guy standing at the bus stop by the Adelphi Hotel in the pouring rain. Knowing the last bus had gone, Rory pulled over and offered the man a lift and he got in. Guapa had been asleep under Rory's jumper, but was awoken by the man chatting and poked her face out. The man commented to Rory: 'You do know that you have an owl down your jumper don't you?', as if an owl was normal to have there. Rory tried to explain, but his stutter stopped him, and Guapa was not going to wait. Out she popped and jumped onto the man's head. He started shouting and Rory stopped the car. The man opened the door and was last seen running up the street screaming. Sadly Guapa became violent around people at home and in the end had to be put down.

The gigs carried on for The Hurricanes, although they had scaled them down due to family commitments. In the summer of 1966 Eileen gave birth to her and Johnny's daughter. Johnny now had extra responsibilities. They were still a great band to watch, thrilling crowds and getting them dancing. Ty and his wife Irene moved into a bungalow in Bradwell Road, Lowton, Warrington, not far from Leigh. Jimmy Tushingham also bought a bungalow in the close, while Jamo put his name down on one that was yet to be built. The three mates were happy to be living near each other. The year 1967 arrived, along with a few more venues for the band. Ty fell ill with appendicitis, and so severe was it that surgeons had to operate on him. Due to his sickness the band would cover Ty, with Karl Terry often taking his place on lead guitar. A bit of mixing around and people lending a hand to fill in got them by. Jimmy Tushingham was finding it tedious that the Hurricanes' sets where not changing, and when an offer came from Vince Earl to join The Connoisseurs, he took it and wished the lads well.

Ty was getting stronger after his operation, playing when he could and resting when he had to. At one gig while Rory was singing, he glanced over and noticed that Ty was sitting on an amp clearly in pain, but still playing. He told Ty to go home, but Ty said they had a second set to do. Rory informed him not to worry about the set as they could play without him, and insisted that he go home as he was not well. Ty took his advice and the band played on without him.

A few days later on 20 February 1967 The Hurricanes were booked to play at a venue near Kirkby, with Ty arranging to meet the rest of the band there. They unloaded their gear and placed it on the stage. Ty had not yet arrived, and as it got near the time of their performance he had still not turned up. The guys did not worry too much as Ty was maybe still feeling unwell. They took to the stage to rock the joint. After playing a few numbers a message was passed to the band, telling them about a phone call that the management had just received. The manager looked as white as a sheet when the lads approached him; it was clear to them that something serious was wrong. Ty had collapsed at his home and was rushed to hospital in Leigh. There had been complications from his operation. They tried to save him, but unfortunately Ty died. The shock blew the guys apart. How could Ty be dead? He was only twenty-six. Ty had died from blood poisoning resulting from a duodenal ulcer. Scar tissue had grown over his bowel causing him his problems. He was so fit and strong that it stunned everyone who knew him.

Charles (Ty) O'Brien.

Jimmy Tushingham went along to see his old pal at the chapel of rest. Jimmy recalled that Ty, or Charlie as he called him, was wearing a red top with a gold collar, and as he looked at his friends face he thought 'you are still so good looking'. Charlie (Ty) was buried in Merseyside. His family have asked for the location of his grave not to be printed within this book and the author has respected and followed their wishes. His coffin was carried by his distraught friends Jimmy, Johnny, Rory and Jamo. Lou Walters was also present at the funeral of his old friend and bandmate. Irene stayed in the house that they had bought together for a few years before she married again. Ty loved the colour red, and for many years after his death his old pal Jamo would lay a red rose on his grave every year on his birthday.

The *Liverpool Echo* reported Ty's death on Thursday 2 March 1967:

Ty Brien, lead guitarist with the Liverpool group Rory Storm and the Hurricanes, has died in hospital at the age of 26. Ty – real name Charles O'Brien – was married only 12 months ago, and had recently moved into a new bungalow in Bradwell Road, Lawton, near Leigh. He was a close friend of Beatle Ringo Starr, who was a member of the same group for 6 years.

Ty had married in 1965, while Ringo was with the band for three years.

Rory and Johnny were heartbroken. Ty was their friend, band member and brother. It was all too much to handle and the shock had numbed them. Without Ty they could not play. The Hurricanes were over. They had agreed to play at the wedding of Rory's friend Pete Vernon on 25 February at the Grafton. Somehow they managed to perform the gig and gave the guest a great show. Pete remembers that one of the songs Rory sang was the Wilson Pickett number 'Land of One Thousand Dancers' and that the band thrilled the guest when they performed it. But that was it, and they informed the other band members that it was over before cancelling any booked gigs. It was now a time for grief and reflection. Rory's sister Iris recalled that when she heard of his death the song playing on the radio was '(They Long To Be) Close To You', and that every time she hears the song she thinks of Ty, or Charlie as she called him.

A few weeks after Ty's death, Rory and Johnny decided to give the band one more try. Ex-The Mojos members Adrian Lord (guitar) and Keith Karlson (bass) joined up with them, along with Carl Rich on drums. Rory and Johnny never really had their hearts in it. Ringo, Lou, and Jimmy leaving the band had knocked them badly, but the death of Ty was far beyond anything they had experienced. The Hurricanes were finished. After all these years it was over. Their last ever public gig took place at the Orrell Park Ballroom.

They had not hit the big time, no chart records came their way, and they had not become household names. However, they had thrilled thousands of people with their bouncing shows and energetic singer, travelled and performed together as great friends, been Liverpool's top band, played alongside some very big names and had a whole lot of fun in the process. They had set the standards in those early days and people had wanted to be just like them. They were a huge part of the Merseyside music scene – a very important part – with their significance often being overlooked. It is said that they missed getting signed up as they did not write their own songs. Yet, a lot of groups went on to have hits with cover versions. The Rolling Stones recorded eight cover singles out of their first ten to be released. The Hurricanes were getting as much work as anybody else in the early 1960s, and while they did stay with Rock 'n' Roll numbers, they did them very well indeed. All the groups signed needed guidance, The Beatles included, and we are left to wonder what might have been if someone had taken a chance on The Hurricanes.

8

Rory Goes It Alone

The Hurricanes were no more. Ringo had become a worldwide star, Charles (Ty) had sadly passed away, Walter (Lou) and Johnny had both married and settled down and Rory was still single and restless. Rory had money saved from his days as a Hurricane, but it would not last forever. He still craved the stage and the limelight, but with no band what could he do? He decided to try out as a DJ, but being Rory he could not be any ordinary DJ. Instead, he would be the singing and dancing DJ. He hired two girl dancers to perform alongside him and they went down pretty well. Once more Rory had all eyes on him. One of his nicknames in his band days was 'The Golden Boy', and Rory used this for the act, calling them 'The Golden Boy and The Golden Girls'.

The Golden Boy and The Golden Girls. Kathy Nagle, on the left, became Rory's girlfriend. (Courtesy of Iris Caldwell)

Rory had not had many long-term girlfriends, though he had no trouble with attracting the ladies. His stammer was the problem, making him embarrassed when speaking to girls. He had been fine as the rock star, with plenty of females interested in the good-looking singer, but when he had tried dating the girls that he liked his stutter would take over. The shame he felt was sickening, and it was easier for him to just spend a few days with a woman then move on before the getting to know each other chats started. Some girls would lose interest when they heard his stutter, while others could not care less about it. It was Rory who hated it, and he removed himself from the situation rather than face it, thus making the problem and fear of shame much worse. Unless you have been a stutterer you have no idea what Rory faced, for it is a vicious affliction that leaves a person feeling frustrated and embarrassed as they attempt one of life's necessities, communication. It is to his credit that Rory refused to allow his stammer to stop him achieving, instead pushing himself into the limelight through athletics and music.

No matter how bad his stutter was in his personal life, he had no option at times but to face it. They say that love conquers all, stammers included, and Rory was to discover this. One of the dancers in his DJ act was a stunning-looking girl called Kathy Nagle, who held a crush for Rory, as he did for her. They were clearly attracted to and fond of one another, and soon began dating. Their romance grew and blossomed. They fell in love,

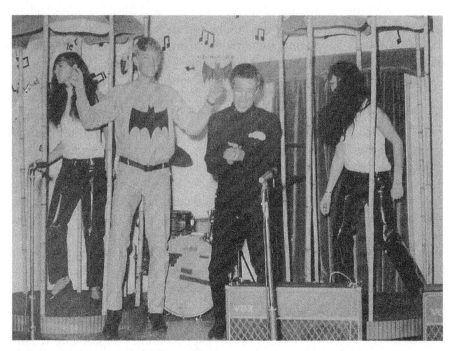

The Golden Boy and The Golden Girls in action. (Courtesy of Iris Caldwell)

and Rory found he could be himself and chat around her. Kathy was not put off by his stutter. She loved Rory and understood the stammer was a part of who he was. From going steady they moved on to an engagement, with plans for a future together. Life was good, and everyone was happy for them – well almost everyone.

Kathy's parents were worried about Rory's choice of work, saying that they would prefer it if their daughter's future husband had a regular and secure job. Kathy finally gave in to her parents and suggested to Rory that he found safer employment. He was horrified at the thought of returning to a desk job like the one he had as a cotton salesman. He was a free spirit, an entertainer, not a nine-to-five robot. Kathy kept on at him and Rory kept giving excuses, so she gave him an option of finding a job or breaking off their engagement. Rory loved her and wanted his future with Kathy. He weighed it all up and decided he would give it a go. He could do what all the other men do and settle. But could the free-spirited Rory really do it?

Any office job was out of the question. He had been there before and hated it. He could drive and that gave him many work choices, and when he heard that taxi drivers were wanted he applied and was taken on. It was hard work but it was a steady job, and he could save for his future with Kathy. On a busy day he pulled his cab over into a space on Lime Street, a policeman telling him to move it as he did so. Rory shouted 'for Christ sake!' but it came out 'ffffffffff' as his stutter took over. The police officer asked him to get out of the cab and arrested him, claiming he had insulted an officer of the law by telling him to 'fuck off'. Rory could not believe this was happening and was even angrier once he found out the police had informed his employer, who then sacked him.

Rory rose above it. Screw them, another job would come – and it did. The Hoylake coastguard rescue team needed a new member. This was more like it. The thrill and adventure 'Rory to the rescue' job was secured and Rory was ready to be a hero. The reality however, found him sitting around waiting for something to happen, cleaning the rescue boat and hoping they had training scheduled so that he could at least get out on the water. Rory had a hyperactive nature; doing nothing was torture to him, and this was worse than a bloody office job. He also had to face the constant questions about Ringo being in his band, The Beatles' fame and why he had not made it. It ground him down and became a nuisance to him. Back home in Old Swan Rory got talking to a man who ran a barber shop on Oakhill Road. Rory had always fancied a try at hairdressing, after all he had created a great style for himself, so when the man offered him a job at the shop he jumped at it. The shop was not far from his home in Broad Green Road. it suited Rory fine, so he packed in his job with the rescue team. He took to hairdressing well, becoming very good at it. This was a job he could do every day for certain.

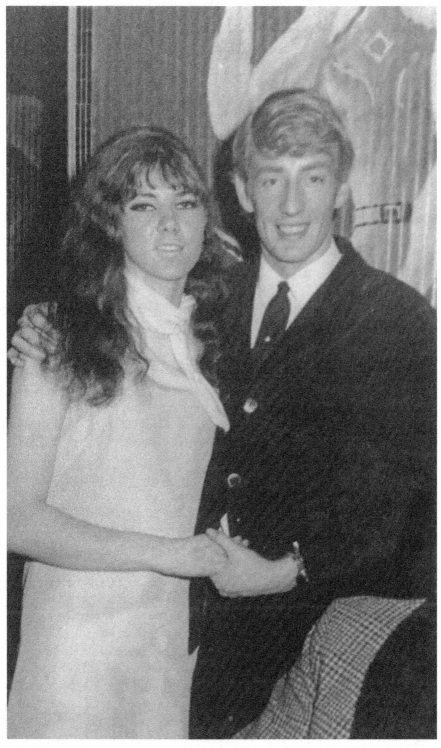

Kathy and Rory. (Courtesy of Iris Caldwell)

Rory and Kathy flew to Majorca for a holiday in the summer of 1969. A postcard sent to Rory's friend Pete Vernon shows they were having a good time:

Dear Pete and Vivian.
    Great here, Beach parties, Barbecues, Bullfights. Both suntanned masses, meet your Mum and dad every night in a great bar. Cheers Rory and Kathy.

Bullfights? It appeared that Rory was intrigued by the prospect of seeing one. Kathy wanted nothing to do with such a cruel sport and told him to go on his own if he really wanted to watch the spectacle. When he returned he looked everywhere for Kathy, but there was no sign of her. Rory walked to the beach, and there he found her, making love to another man. He flew home feeling dejected and betrayed; he wanted nothing more to do with Kathy.

The manager at the barber shop told him he would have to let him go, explaining that he was great at his job, but that a number of the customers had refused to have him cut their hair due to his stutter. Once more the stutter had messed things up for him. He was down, but not out, and bounced back up fighting. He took a job as a door-to-door salesman – very difficult for someone with a stutter, but that was Rory, always up for a challenge. He hated it, though it was one of the few times his stutter came in handy as people tended to buy things from him as soon as he started to speak. When one lady asked him if he was Faron from Faron and The Flamingos, it was the final straw. Rory was fed up with Liverpool and fancied taking off abroad somewhere. Benidorm looked like a good idea. A flight was booked, his Vauxhall Cresta was sold, and off he went, finding himself somewhere to stay and a job as a DJ. He loved it, the endless sun, the ladies, the fun, and no mention of The Beatles. Rory took a day job teaching people to water ski, and would also thrill the crowds with spectacular dives from the high rocks into the sea.

Rory became friends with a German guy from Düsseldorf called Bernd and his English girlfriend Elaine. They worked as an acrobatic team and formed a good friendship with Rory. They would also later perform on the same show with Rory's sister Iris in Barcelona. When the holiday season was over, Rory bought the Chevrolet Impala car from his two friends and realised that he could not take it back to the UK until he had owned it for a year. His sister Iris was working in Amsterdam as a dancer with her husband's band Shane Fenton and The Fentones, so he decided to pay them a visit, driving through Spain, France and Belgium to reach The Netherlands. Rory knew that they had a short contract at a club called The Blue Note in Amsterdam and made his way there when

Rory diving into the sea from the rocks in Benidorm. (Courtesy of Iris Caldwell)

he arrived in the city. Iris was delighted to see her brother, with she and Shane telling him he was welcome to stay at their apartment. Rory was delighted. Not only was he able to spend time with his sister but his baby nephew as well, babysitting for them when they worked at night.

Amsterdam was known for its rather seedy side, so Shane and Iris had hired three topless go-go dancers to perform with the band. It was not long before Rory had bedded all three of them. In February of 1971, Violet was interviewed by the *Liverpool Daily Post* for a feature about being the mother of a pop star:

> He had a guitar when he was 17, and came home to ask me if his friend could come in and rehearse. He and his pals formed a group and tried to think of a name. They thought of 'Dracula and The Werewolves' Then the 'Tornadoes' and then decided on 'The Hurricanes'. Ringo Starr was the drummer, and they went on the Carol Levis show and made a hit. This was about 1960, and from there they went to Butlins at Pwllheli. Oh! The excitement. It was as if they had won the Irish sweep-stake.

Rory put his DJ skills to good use and found a job at the Lucky Star nightclub. When Iris and Shane returned to Liverpool he rented an attic flat. He liked Amsterdam, and he was staying. The children in the area liked the Englishman and his big American car, and Rory was happy to let them play in it and take them for drives. His life in Amsterdam was much more laid-back than in Liverpool, and it suited him. In the summer of 1971 Ernie and Vi came over to visit. Rory showed them the sights and took his mother dancing in a local disco. They had a wonderful time and were happy for their son, even though they missed him not living at home. But Rory was settled: good job, good money, good life. He even spoke Dutch – only a little, but it was coming along well.

Rory made a phone call to Sam Leach in Liverpool. When Sam answered the phone he heard an excited Rory say 'Sam! Sam! Listen, I can speak clear.' Rory was delighted, as Sam was for him. It turned out that a friend of Rory's in Amsterdam had told him that he was going to punch him in the arm every time he stuttered, and the threat of pain had eased his stammer somewhat. Probably it was his new lifestyle and happiness that really helped his speech.

Ernie was hoping for promotion to head porter at Broadgreen hospital. He was in line to get it and it would bring a few more pounds into the family kitty. He was walking the long corridor at the hospital when he felt dizzy and dropped to his knees. A voice asked was he OK, and as he looked up he saw the lady who was making the decision on who got the head porter job. Ernie said he was fine and was looking for a shilling he had dropped. The lady told him 'no you are not', and called for help. Ernie was put in a bed on a ward and tests were done. Everything came

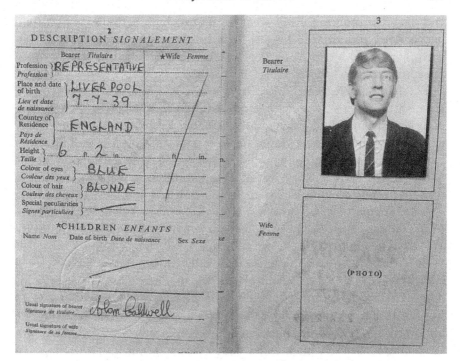

Rory's passport. He changed his age and birthdate. Using number 7, he could say the second 7 was a 1 if questioned. (Courtesy of Iris Caldwell)

back fine. Vi and Iris were so worried about him, Iris was in fact a week away from giving birth to her second child.

On Friday 28 January Ernie was getting ready to go home. The curtains were drawn around his bed as he got dressed, with the man in the next bed commenting on how cheerful he sounded. Ernie replied 'Why not? I have the best wife, two best kids and Jesus in my life.' As the man next to him chatted away he noticed that Ernie had gone quiet, so he climbed out of his bed and pulled back the curtains to find Ernie on the floor. Help was called and it was discovered that he had a blood clot on his brain that had caused a stroke. His family arrived and sat with him, and Rory was contacted in Amsterdam.

Rory returned to his flat to be greeted by a telegram, telling him his father Ernie had suffered a stroke and was in hospital. Ernie was in a serious condition and had fallen into a coma. Rory tried to get a flight home, but could not get one until Monday 31 January. When he landed in Liverpool his brother-in-law Shane was there to meet him. Rory got in the car and talked away about Amsterdam and the work he was doing, with Shane trying to interrupt him to tell him the news. Rory talked until the car pulled up at the house on Broad Green Road, then he said to Shane 'So, how is he then?' Shane then had to tell him that his father had died that morning. Rory went to the Craven funeral home on Broad Green Road and sat with his father in the chapel of rest for many hours. It really affected him as they were so close and Ernie had doted so much after his son.

The family were heartbroken by the loss of Ernie. Rory was worried about his mother's mental state. She had suffered problems before, and with her husband gone how would she cope? He made a decision to stay in Liverpool, but Vi insisted that he went back to Amsterdam, telling him that Iris and Shane were only minutes away in Oakhill Park, and that she had plenty of friends. Rory agreed. Pete Vernon took Rory for a drink in the Queens pub on Queens Drive. He remembered that Rory was wearing a short fur coat that had no arms. Rory told him he would be going back to Amsterdam and asked Pete to get a seaman's ticket and join him. Pete explained he could not as he was married.

Rory returned to Amsterdam by air only to find the nightclub closed and his job gone. He set off in his car for the ferry port. Jersey was his destination. Rory had been offered a job as a DJ at the New Plaza Club in Saint Helier and was going to take up the offer – another new lifestyle beckoned. He still worried about his mother, calling her every day, with her telling him to live his life and not to worry so much. It was all going so well in Saint Helier, they liked him there, and he was finding some happiness after the loss of his father. He had a good circle of friends, hanging out with the likes of DJ Chris Sparkes, known as Sparky, Norman Hale, the great piano and organ player who had played with The Tornados, and Joyce and Hughie Behan, who had bought the West Park Pavilion and turned it into a successful venue under the name 'Behans'. Rory was hanging out here a lot, often getting up to perform.

However, one evening in May 1972 he was set upon by a gang who had overheard his Scouse accent. Rory was beaten up badly and was finished with Jersey. On his arrival back in Liverpool he noticed that his mother's depression was returning, and he let her know that he would be staying as this is where he wanted to be.

Violet's mental health was worsening. The doctors had given her pills and were considering electric therapy treatment. Vi was terrified at the thought of this; she still held the memories of her previous course of the treatment, and while it had helped it had also been an horrific experience. Rory was extremely worried about his mother and would not leave her. When friends called he told them he would love to sing in a band or return to his cabaret DJ act, but he had to help his mother. He had to make sure that she took her pills, and help her get over his father's death and her illness. He hardly left the house. Iris and Shane would call around and were worried about both Vi and Rory. Violet's depression had worsened; she would say that she died the day that Ernie did. Rory was spending all day of every day experiencing his mother this way, which pulled him into

The stamps on Rory's passport that show he entered Spain on 28 June 1972. Also, note his return to Amsterdam after his father's death, and a 1970 entry into Ibiza. (Courtesy of Iris Caldwell)

his own depression. Friends tried to help him by getting him out, but he would have none of it, saying that he needed to take care of his mother.

Rory had been suffering from bronchitis, and Iris and Shane asked him to come to Barcelona with them when they found work there as it would help his chest. He agreed and went out with them, pitching a tent next to the caravan they were staying in. So, the many stories that appear in books claiming Rory stayed in his house after returning from Jersey are simply untrue. Unfortunately, the man who had hired them was arrested for drug offences and their contract was cancelled, meaning that they had to return to Liverpool, where Rory once more hardly ventured outside his house. Iris remains convinced that had they stayed in Spain, things would have turned out different for Rory.

Iris was becoming more and more worried about her brother. His stutter was getting worse and he was becoming paranoid about it after working in Jersey where he had suffered a lot of abuse because of it. Iris told him that they could buy a van and a load of second-hand clothes and go around the new estates in Liverpool selling them. He could drive and she would do the talking, then they could form a duo together and go back on stage. Rory agreed to it all.

His good friend Pete Vernon did get him to attend Liverpool FC's first game of the season at Anfield on 12 August, and Rory enjoyed the 2-0 win against Manchester City. But after that Rory started refusing phone calls and knocks on the door by getting his mother to say he was out. Pete had gone to a wedding reception at The Old Stanley pub in Old Swan. When he went into the pub he noticed Ringo Starr was there as one of the guests and quickly ran to a nearby phone box to ring Rory. Vi answered and Pete told her that he would come and get him as he would love to see Ringo again. Vi said Rory was out, so he never got to see his old friend again. Of course Rory was at home – Pete knew it – and his worry for him just grew more.

Pete Vernon saw Rory on 25 September, had a chat, and asked him if he would like to do something the following day. Rory told him that he had arranged to play golf with his Uncle Eric that day, so not to bother. Eric had not booked anything with Rory, so it seems like this was another excuse to avoid going out. Rory also had bad tooth trouble, resulting in a visit to the dentist for treatment on 26 September. He returned home, took painkillers and put himself to bed. Vi had been to visit her daughter Iris around the corner in Oakhill Park, before returning to the family home. While there she had baked a cake with Iris for one of the children. Iris was so excited that she kept opening the oven to look at the cake and in the end the air made it fall flat. Vi started laughing and Iris started crying. 'Why are you crying?' Vi asked her daughter. 'Because it is the first time I have seen you laugh since dad died,' replied Iris. They hugged and Vi told Iris that she loved her and would always be there for her.

Wednesday 27 September 1972 was just another day; people went to work, children went to school, shops closed for half a day. Vi would visit her sister Doris on a Wednesday and they would go to the library. Doris waited but Vi never showed. Iris was taking an evening class at Winnie Mac's opposite her mother's house. She noticed that the lights were out in the house, but had no worries as her mother would be at her sister's house and Rory was probably watching the football on TV at Pete Vernon's. The class ended and the lights were still off. Iris made her way to her house in Oakhill Park. At home, Iris reached for the bucket to clean the babies' nappies, and as she did a feeling came over her that both her mother and brother were dead. She could not ring her Aunty Doris as she had no phone, but she rang Pete Vernon who told her they had not been to his house. Iris said, 'I think they are dead Pete', and he told her not to be silly, they will be with Doris. Iris then phoned Winnie Mac and asked her to go and knock at their door. She came back on the phone and said that no lights were on, the *Echo* newspaper was still in the letter box, and Rory's car was in the garage (it was an open-front garage). Iris now panicked. Shane was out at a gig and she asked Winnie to send her daughter to mind her children, before running around to her mother's house.

Winnie Mac was on the step of the house with next door neighbours Tom and Esta. Iris took the spare key from under the plant pot and Tom opened the door. They all then walked into the living room. On the table sat two fresh cream cakes and forty cigarettes, and the house was cleaned spotless. Iris again said that they were dead. Tom found a note left by Vi and told Iris to stay in the living room, before climbing the stairs. In the back bedroom he found Rory with a sheet pulled up over his face. Tom tried to shake him, but it was clear that he was dead. Tom went into the main bedroom where he found Violet in her bed. Sadly she had also passed away. He went back downstairs and informed Iris that he could not wake them, before calling the police.

The police arrived at the house and conducted searches of the property, checking for signs of intruders and gathering up the medicine bottles. Tom and Esta took Iris into their house next door. A paramedic arrived and informed Iris that her mother and brother were both dead. Iris grabbed him by the collars and shouted 'Tell me! Tell me!' The man kept saying 'I am sorry love, they are dead.' What he was saying was not sinking in for Iris, even though she knew it was true. Later, a strange locum doctor arrived and asked who had shot them; he certainly had been given the wrong information.

The bodies of Violet and Rory where moved to hospital in the early hours of 28 September. A post-mortem on both would be needed. The result was that Rory had not taken enough tablets to kill himself. Instead, he had taken sleeping tablets and a tiny amount of whiskey in the hope of getting some sleep. He had breathing problems, a painful tooth, and was hypo. He just wanted to sleep, and his body was so weak that it appears the tablets knocked him out and his body gave up and died. It seems that Violet discovered her son's death and performed her last actions as a loving and caring mother by covering her sons face with the sheet. She then drank a number of glasses of whiskey and took a large amount of pills. The sadness of finding her son dead had been too much for her.

Iris remains adamant that Rory had not taken his own life. He was a showman who would have done it in style, at least leaving a note and not wearing his pyjamas in bed. Plus cream cakes and forty cigarettes are not what you buy if you are planning to end your life, so Vi must have returned from the shops, checked on Rory and found he had died. A verdict of accidental death was recorded for Rory – while of unstable mind. The post-mortem is all anybody who claims that Rory took his own life needs to read. It is there in black and white: he did not take enough tablets to kill himself. Violet had written a note asking for people to forgive them and to pray for them. Maybe she had believed that Rory had taken his own life? The absolute truth of what happened in that house will never be

One of the author's favourite photographs – Rory as a young boy in his back garden. (Courtesy of Iris Caldwell)

known. What is more important is that two wonderful, kind, and caring individuals had passed away. The local press made Rory headline news, this time, sadly, for all the wrong reasons. The death certificate for Rory records his name as Alan Caldwell, which also indicates he did not change his name by deed poll but adopted Rory Storm.

The press arrived in force. Iris had been sedated, and Shane dealt with them by hosting a press conference. Iris explained that most wrote fitting tributes to Rory and Vi except for *The Sun*, who decided to write a disgusting story suggesting Rory and Vi were in bed together – absolutely shameful on them. They also never attended the press conference, instead deciding to write sensational rubbish. When Iris read *The Sun*'s story it tore her apart. She went along to the Press club in Liverpool city centre, where the man at the door asked her for her badge, saying 'You need one to get in here.' Iris replied, 'Do you need one to walk all over somebody's feelings?' Two men sitting at the bar came over and one asked her if she was Rory's sister. They told her they had been discussing the story in *The Sun*, and along with other journalists were sickened by it. The newspaper was contacted and an explanation was asked for. They said they would print an apology, but it never happened. Iris has never bought that paper since that day, and their behaviour over the Hillsborough tragedy has only strengthened her resolve never to buy it.

The funeral of Violet and Rory was handled by Craven, with both Rory and Vi resting in their chapel. Iris could not face going in to see them, so she would sit on a chair outside the room and talk to them through the open door. The funeral took place on 4 October, and the service was held at the family church of All Saints on Broad Green Road with mourners packing the aisles, many of them members of Merseybeat bands. Johnny Guitar carried the coffin of his friend, the boy he had met on a bus in 1956 and dreamed the dream with. Vince Earl and Jimmy Tushingham also acted as pall-bearers for their old band member, alongside Pete Vernon and Sam Leach. Lou Walters also attended the funeral. The coffins were carried side by side into the church, and as they entered Rory's favourite song was sung by those gathered – 'You'll Never Walk Alone'. The Revd Peter Beaman said of Rory, 'He should be remembered for his skill at athletics and for his contribution to the entertainment world and to the happiness of others.' He also praised Violet for the endless encouragement she had shown her son. After the service they moved on to Anfield crematorium, with their ashes being placed in plot twenty-three.

Later the mourners were invited back to Iris's house in Oakhill Park, where she played a tape of Rory singing songs that he was thinking of using in his cabaret act. None of The Beatles attended the funeral, but how could they? It would have been a media circus. Kathy Nagle, Rory's ex-fiancée, attended his funeral. She came over in tears to the car that Iris was in and spoke to her. While Rory was in the chapel of rest in Cravens funeral parlour on Broad Green Road, someone put a red rose by his coffin every day, and Iris believes it was Kathy who did it.

Rory's old roadie and pal Jamo was unaware of his death. Jamo, who was working as an car engineer for the police force at the time, had taken a police car to get spare parts. As he walked into the parts office the guy behind the counter said 'I see your mate's getting buried today.' Jamo asked who he meant and was floored when the guy told him that it was Rory. Jamo rang his boss to explain about the funeral and was told to take a car and go. He arrived at the church in a police car and was still dressed in his work overalls, but he had made it for his old friend.

The Beatles press officer Derek Taylor told the *Liverpool Echo*

He was a first-class band leader, quite apart from his singing ability. The last time we met was in 1964, when the late Brian Epstein brought him and his group to London to record 'America' It was a first-class piece of work, but unfortunately didn't make the charts. His mum was just as involved in the band as he was, and I think, sometimes that she was the one who kept him going.

Iris went to visit a fortune-teller in the Old Swan tenement flats. Her name was Kitty and she was bedridden, with pictures of Jesus and the saints around her bed. She told Iris she could see two coffins side by side, and that her mum wanted her to know that she was with her brother Len. Iris was stunned. All her mother had ever wanted was to see her brother Len again. Iris continued to visit Kitty, who later asked her why she was leaving Liverpool. Confused, Iris told her she was not going anywhere, and Kitty replied 'You will be living in London, and your husband will be on stage with women admiring him, but he will have a different name.' Not long afterwards, Shane was given a contract and moved with his family to London. He also changed his stage name to Alvin Stardust and went on to have a number of chart hits. Kitty was correct again. Iris kept in touch with Kitty, phoning her from time to time. One day when she called Kitty asked her how her son liked his new big ball. Iris was once again stunned, for the previous day she had bought her son a big ball to play with. Iris has always wondered if Ringo had got Rory to work on the film *That'll Be The Day* as a consultant (because it was really taken from his life at Butlins), would he have had a reason to rally round and find a niche for his talent again?

The beautiful blue-eyed boy was dead, and this fact had touched many people. The crazy singer, who had thrilled and entertained so many, was now gone, but he could never be forgotten – he was far too memorable for that. Just a few months after his death, the single 'America' went to number one in Texas, USA, which he would have loved. Rory had died just before Glam Rock had taken off. He would have been perfect for this, and let's face it, he had been doing it years before anyone else. A lot of people within the Merseyside music scene have commented about the singer Rod Stewart, and of how when they first saw him they also saw Rory's act: the wild blonde hair and crazy clothes, even the gold boots that Rory had worn. Many are convinced that Rod must have seen Rory perform as it is just too uncanny.

Liverpool had lost a legend: a baby who sat in a shelter with his parents as the enemy planes attacked; a boy who played on bomb sites and lit fires so that he could see the fire engines arrive; one who refused to allow a stammer to keep him down; the athlete, sportsman, singer, entertainer; the caring guy who would do anything for anyone; the nice guy and the dreamer who dared to dream. Rory had done it all, but, most importantly, in a nice way. The King of Liverpool fits him like no other.

9

Hurricanes Till This Day

Ringo Starr went on to international fame with The Beatles, and his life is so well documented that it would make little sense writing it here. However, he will be mentioned again towards the end of this book. Ty (Charlie) had tragically passed away in 1967. His parents, Charles and Marie, continued to live at the house in Pemberton Road until Marie's death in 1983. Charles later emigrated to Canada to live with his daughter.

Johnny Guitar was already married with a daughter by the time The Hurricanes called it a day, and took a job as a taxi driver. In 1970 he and Eileen had been blessed with a son. With a young family to support, Johnny changed jobs and became a milkman, later becoming an ambulance driver then an emergency medical technician with the ambulance service, working from Crosby ambulance station. He was very good at his job and well liked, telling colleagues about his time as a Hurricane and showing them bits of his memorabilia collection. Ever the rock star and as cool as ever, he wore his leather jacket to and from work. The crew were a close bunch; the banter would flow, and they would attend meet ups for gigs and parties.

Johnny had amassed a huge collection of tickets, posters, newspaper clippings, badges and photographs from his time playing as a Hurricane, plus numerous items connected to other bands from the Merseybeat scene. He would display and sell some of his items at The Beatles festivals in Liverpool. In the 1990s Johnny formed the band Johnny Guitar and The Hurricanes, to play at events organised for charity. He still played the Antoria guitar that he had bought in 1959 and it still sounded great. He remained a Rock 'n' Roll star and could still thrill the crowds.

Johnny had also kept a diary between the years 1958 and 1963. It gave a good insight into playing with a band during the rise of the Beat era on Merseyside. When it was made public it allowed readers a glimpse into history, letting them follow The Hurricanes from their birth as a

Skiffle band to their arrival as one of the top groups in Liverpool. With the inclusion of gigs, wages, instruments, cars, girls, touring and much more, it surely has to be one of the most important documents from the Liverpool music scene.

A short documentary was made about Rory storm and The Hurricanes on the programme *A Day In The Life*, which featured Johnny talking about the old days with the band. During it Johnny tells of Rory during the 'Beat and Bathe Night' in New Brighton, how he climbed to the top of the diving board and stripped down to tiny gold shorts – Rory could not be seen in normal shorts – and executed a triple somersault with perfect landing, after which he got out the pool and continued the song. Johnny added, 'You couldn't follow that.' It is noticeable how much Johnny smiles as he talks about his old friend Rory; his love for him clearly comes through. The film then moves on to Johnny playing as Johnny and The Hurricanes. He explains that they still did the same numbers that Rory had sung – no special effects, just authentic Rock 'n' Roll.

Johnny and Eileen drifted apart and the marriage ended in divorce. In the summer of 1984 he remarried, to Margaret Ritchie, and they settled in Stuart Road in Crosby. Walter Eymond had attended Johnny's wedding. Sadly he was diagnosed with motor neurone disease and had to retire from the ambulance service. Although ill, Johnny continued performing for the Merseycats and Merseyrats charities alongside other band members and singers from the Beat era. A number of clips of Johnny and the band playing have appeared on YouTube over the years. As his illness took over, it left Johnny unable to play the guitar, which he hated. On 14 November 1998, Johnny got up on stage at his retirement party. His guitar had a kind of rest added to it for his right hand to sit on. He could no longer strum, but he shaped the chords with his left hand as he sang 'Some Other Guy'. A few months later, on 14 May 1999, he appeared at the 'Merseycats Tenth Anniversary Show' at Bootle Town Hall. His guitar had to be almost tied to his body to keep it on him, but he got up on stage and did his stuff – an absolute trooper. It was one of Johnny's final performances.

Just weeks later, on 18 August 1999, Johnny collapsed at his home and died. The guy who had lived and breathed Rock 'n' Roll had passed away at the age of fifty-nine. His funeral took place on 24 August with over 300 people in attendance, including his first wife Eileen. Many people mentioned that they had not seen so many musicians from the Merseybeat groups at a funeral since Rory had died in 1972, which says everything about these two likeable lads. Johnny's ashes were placed in the Thornton garden of rest on Lydiate Lane. Obituaries for Johnny appeared in *The Guardian* and *The Independent*. His family and close friends were devastated, and the music world, especially in Merseyside, was stunned by the loss of this likeable and popular man.

Lou had married Yeolande Madeira in 1964, and by early 1965 had left The Hurricanes. Lou formed a band called 'Combo' with Brian Griffiths from The Big Three, and the band were based on the Wirral. Lou played bass and sang main vocals while Brian played lead guitar. They were joined by a drummer, keyboarder and saxophonist. They played a mixture of music from ballads to Rock 'n' Roll, with a few John Lee Hooker numbers thrown in, though they always opened a set with the Booker T. & the M. G.'s hit 'Green onions'. The band proved very popular on the circuit and found regular venues in Frodsham and Runcorn. The members chopped and changed, and later they recruited a new bass player so that Lou could front the band as a singer. Combo played around the North West area until they called it a day in 1972.

That same year Lou was taken on as the under manager and MC at the Bulls Head in Little Sutton – wage packet, national insurance, the full deal. One evening Lou noticed a guy watching him from the side of the stage. When Lou came off the guy approached him and told him he was a tax officer and he knew that he was not paying tax on this job. Lou told him to get lost, before the manager came out with Lou's contract. 'There you go,' said the manager as he showed him the contract, quickly followed by 'now the doors that way, get out before my boot kicks you through it.'

Lou's parents had moved to Chester, and with him being based on the Wirral he followed with Yeolande. Their daughter was born here in 1970. He trained as a psychiatric nurse before finding work at the Deva Hospital in Chester. With the job came a house at No. 18 Bach Hall Estate, which Lou and Yoelande later bought. In 1974 a second daughter was born to the couple, who raised their children at Bach Hall for many years before moving on to another address. The couple later split and divorced. Yeolande sadly passed away in 2001.

Walter is now retired and is a great-grandfather. His family are extremely proud of his association with The Hurricanes. Walter played a huge part in the history of the band, as well as playing with other top groups from the era. He was a great bass player, who gave us a number of musical firsts. He was the first man from Liverpool to play and own an electric bass, and was the singer on the legendary, and lost, recordings that were made at the Akustik studio in Hamburg – the first time that all four future Beatles came together to record. Walter was also the first person who made Cilla Black get up on a stage to sing. History has a lot to thank him for.

In 1973 the film *That'll Be The Day* was released. It featured David Essex as the wannabe rock star, with Ringo Starr taking the part of a fairground attendant. Billy Fury played a character named Stormy Tempest, which is clearly a play on the name of Rory Storm. Ringo also looks very much a Teddy Boy in the film, as he did when he played with

The Hurricanes. Having had Ringo as their drummer, and being friends and rivals of Lennon, McCartney and Harrison, The Hurricanes have ensured their mention in just about every book that has been written about The Beatles. But they are far more than just the band that Ringo played with, as is implied many times in print. If anything they improved Ringo and brought him into the limelight by giving him his own slot and songs to sing. They were also a very good band in their own right, putting on a great stage show, and this is far too often overlooked by some Beatles authors.

Being a group who recorded so little material, they would often fall into the 'also ran' category. But it is impossible to keep a band such as The Hurricanes down, and they would keep popping back up. A musical about them called 'The Need For Heroes: The Story of Rory Storm' was performed at the Neptune theatre in their home city in 1987. Sitting in the audience watching the play was the actor Carl Wharton. As he watched, something in his head told him 'I will play that character one day.' Carl had no idea just how correct his thoughts were to be, nor did he have any kind of inkling that the writer and producer Slim Parry was at that very moment staring at Carl instead of the play thinking, 'Now that guy could play Rory Storm.'

A few years later Slim came in search of Carl and told him about a play that he had written about Rory and the band. He explained that he had seen Carl sitting in the audience that day and wanted to know if he was interested in trying out for the part of Rory Storm. Carl said he was and a meeting with the musicians who would be playing the band members was arranged. When Carl arrived they asked him if he could sing? He explained he had sung in plays but never as a frontman. They then asked if he knew any Rock 'n' Roll songs. 'Not really,' replied Carl. When they suggested 'Blue Suede Shoes' Carl told them that he knew some of the words and it was agreed he would try it out. He was offered the part and accepted it straight away.

I must give my admiration to Carl. Here was a guy who had never sung lead in a band and had no great knowledge of Rock 'n' Roll, who had agreed to take on the part of one of the greatest stage performers that Merseyside had ever produced. I could well imagine many trained and experienced singers turning down the role of Rory Storm out of fear of failure. Remember, Rory was a first-class performer, so fair play to Carl for taking on such a challenging role. Could he pull it off?

Slim Parry had done his research on Rory and passed the details on to Carl. He had a couple of records and a short TV clip to go with the photographs and stories in books. Jamo Jamieson arranged for Carl to meet with Johnny Guitar, who had formed 'Johnny and The Hurricanes' and 'The New Hurricanes' to play at local charity events. Johnny talked to Carl and explained how Rory would perform. He also asked Carl to

Carl Wharton and the band from the play *The King of Liverpool*. (Courtesy of Carl Wharton)

sing a few songs with the band as they still played the numbers that Rory had sung. Carl was stunned. Here was a Merseybeat legend who was happy to take a back seat from singing to give him a chance.

Carl knew that playing Rory would involve a lot more than just singing. He needed to move around a stage and put on a show. Being very fit enabled Carl to perform Rory's high-kicks and exude his stage energy. He also added a few bits of his own, including the splits that Rory never did. But Carl, along with health and safety, drew the line at jumping from balconies onto the stage.

The members of the band needed to be fitted out in the correct clothes for the show. Duncan Classic Tailors on London Road had made the turquoise-and-red suits for The Hurricanes in 1960, and the band had posed outside the shop wearing them. Slim Parry arranged for the guys from the show to go there for a fitting, and the man who had made those original suits all those years before now remade them for the cast members. Of course the opportunity was taken to pose outside the shop, just as The Hurricanes had done. Johnny Guitar gave Carl a pair of his own Chelsea boots to go with his stage suit. Carl still has the boots, along with the suits from the play.

The show 'The King of Liverpool', performed by the Threadbare Theatre Co., opened at the Playhouse theatre in Liverpool early in 1992. It had originally been planned to run for two nights, but it proved so

Carl Wharton as Rory Storm with The Hurricanes. (Courtesy of Carl Wharton)

popular that it ran for two weeks. The play was also performed at the Edinburgh Festival as well as in a number of cities in the UK. By late 1992 it returned for a few shows around Merseyside venues under the title 'Beautiful Dreamer'. Carl also went on to perform as Rory with Johnny Guitar and The New Hurricanes on many occasions, as well as filling the role with the Rory Story Experience band.

Carl had met Rory's sister Iris after performing as her brother at the Liverpool Playhouse. Iris had watched the show and wanted to congratulate Carl on his portrayal of Rory. She told him that she was impressed that he had copied the nose touching that Rory had done at times, and Carl informed her that he had no idea that he had been doing it. Before a show, Carl would sit in his dressing room and talk to Rory, asking him to help him with the performance if he could. At one show Carl was singing and noticed two ladies sitting in the front row crying. As the play went on he noticed that their tears continued. After the show, the two ladies came to thank Carl. They informed him that they had followed Rory and the guys back in the 1960s, and that Carl had played him very well. One of the ladies then explained that she was a medium, and told Carl that the reason she and her friend had been reduced to tears was because she could see Rory in his white suit standing next to Carl on stage. Whether true or not, that gave Carl the shivers, but also a content feeling.

Carl has received many great reviews for his role as Rory Storm, and he admits that it is his favourite part that he has played on a stage. Perhaps the finest tribute to Carl came from Johnny Guitar himself when he said 'When Carl played with the band he convinced me that he was Rory. It was very uncanny and felt like I was watching and listening to a ghost.' Praise indeed.

The name Rory Storm and The Hurricanes sits proudly on the Cavern wall of fame. On 27 September 1992 'Rorytania' was held at the Montrose Club in Liverpool as a tribute to Rory on the twentieth anniversary of his death. The name Rorytania had come from the 1974 Bob Wooler poem that was written in tribute of Rory. The Merseycats put on a great show and tribute to their old friend, with bands playing including The Dominoes, Ian and The Zodiacs, and Gus Travis and The Midnighters. Johnny Guitar was also in attendance, performing with The New Hurricanes.

Liverpool was chosen as the Capital of Culture in 2008, with Ringo Starr returning to his city of birth to perform on the roof of St George's Hall. He sang his song 'Liverpool 8', named after the area of the city where he was born and grew up. In the song, Ringo sang of playing at Butlins with his friend Rory, a nice mention to his former bandmate. Ringo has mentioned the band on many occasions over the years in interviews, and appears to be rather proud of his days as a Hurricane. In 1992 when he visited the rebuilt Cavern club, Ringo signed his name on the squares of both The Beatles and The Hurricanes.

In 2010 it was announced that a film would be made about the band, with the headline 'For forty years, every band has wanted to be bigger than the Beatles. This is the true story of the one band that was ... and its leader, Rory Storm.' Sadly the film never came about; it was rumoured that the makers were put off by the story's ending. Sadly that is what happened, and a true story would have to include the sad untimely deaths. Mentions of a film have again resurfaced since 2010, so maybe the boys will get the movie that they so justly deserve.

The 2010 animated film *The Illusionist* is a story about a down on his luck stage magician in the late 1950s who often has to play second fiddle to other acts on the same bill as him. One of these acts is 'Billy Boy and The Britoons' who bear an uncanny resemblance to Rory Storm and The Hurricanes. Billy Boy is the singer with the big blonde quiff who dances with the microphone stand and rolls around the floor. The drummer has a thin beard, as Ringo did when he was a Hurricane. The bass player looks like Ty, while the guitarist looks like Lou – he is even wearing glasses. Of course the guitars have been swapped around and there is no Johnny, but it leaves you wondering whether the filmmakers had the Hurricanes in mind when they created *The Britoons*.

Rory in diving pose with hair combed to perfection. He was a very talented swimmer and diver. (Courtesy of Iris Caldwell)

In 2012 Dutch writer, journalist and TV presenter Tom Egbers released a book titled *Rory Storm, The King of Liverpool Dethroned by The Beatles*. It tells the story of Rory's life from birth to death, including many photographs and story contributions from Rory's sister Iris. Egbers

Rory Storm. (Courtesy of Iris Caldwell)

fittingly describes Rory as 'The flamboyant front soldier of the musical revolution'. The book makes good reading and brings the story of one of Liverpool's most popular characters to life. Published in Dutch, a translated English version will hopefully be released in the near future.

Also in 2012, Rockstar records released a CD album titled 'Live At The Jive Hive', which featured a recording made of Rory Storm and The Hurricanes on Saturday 5 March 1960 at the Jive Hive Hall in Crosby, Liverpool. The tracks on the CD include 'Brand New Cadillac (You're So Square')', 'Baby I Don't Care', 'Make Me Know You're Mine', 'Bye Bye Love', 'Jet Black', 'Down the Line', 'C'mon Everybody', 'Don't Bug Me Baby', 'Rip It Up', 'Somethin' Else', 'Train to Nowhere', 'Since You Broke My Heart', 'Honey Don't', 'All American Boy' and 'Willie and the Hand Jive'. Also on the tape and included on the CD are four recordings made in Rory's home at No. 54 Broad Green Road – you can hear the band practicing talking to the crowd at Butlins after singing. The songs are 'Milk Cow Blues', 'What'd I Say', 'Cathy's Clown' and 'Now Is The Hour'. A special guest can be heard singing on 'Milk Cow Blues', Rory's budgerigar called Beauty, who was clearly a fan of the band. A recording of The Hurricanes with Rory singing 'Lend Me Your Comb' has also surfaced, believed to have been recorded in Manchester in 1962. Their version of 'Green Onions' has also emerged, and Rory can be heard speaking the introduction to Johnny Guitar. Sadly, the recordings that we know they made of the songs 'Skinnie Minnie', 'Let's Stomp',

Rory and his sister Iris. This is her favourite photograph of the two of them together. (Courtesy of Iris Caldwell)

'A Shot of Rhythm and Blues', 'Talkin about you', 'Ubangi Stomp' and 'I'll Be There' have yet to be found and appear lost, but never say never.

Iris Caldwell had found the tape in a box of items that had once belonged to her brother. They are an important piece of history as they are the earliest known recordings of a complete set by a Merseybeat band. For a recording made in a hall over fifty years previous, they are in very good condition. Thankfully they have now been preserved. While the guitars are sometimes out of tune – the drumming goes a little hectic at times, and Rory's voice is looking for a key on occasions – it is still a good set with plenty of rocking. It also offers a rare glimpse into history.

Rory really stands out, with his voice sounding Punk Rock and Garage at times (remember, this is 1960). There is no sign of his stutter as he introduces the songs in his Scouse/American accent, and he is clearly confident on the stage. Walter Eymond (Lou Walters) proves his singing ability on a couple of the numbers. The music is very raw and crisp – unpolished, but real music – even with a few bum notes at times. It is also recorded before any Merseyside group had gone out to Hamburg, and we know that they all came back much better bands due to the long hours playing there. The earliness of the recording makes it even more special, and while it was recorded using basic equipment, it is a good sound from the very early days of Beat music.

Another factor of the recording is the drumming – is it Ringo? The arguments will continue as to if it is him or not, even though he has said it is not him. Oddly, Ringo did say it was recorded after he had joined The Beatles, but he must be mistaken on that account as it is clearly earlier than August 1962. On the Wednesday before the recording Ringo missed the gig at the Jive Hive as he had flu – Don Singleton filled in for him. The recording was three days later, so was he well enough or did Don fill in again, or maybe another drummer? Iris Caldwell had her birthday on 6 March and recalled in an interview how she remembered all of The Hurricanes, including Ringo, singing happy birthday to her. This was the day after the recording and Ringo was well enough to be out then. Backbeat drumming can be heard on some of the songs, but does that mean that it is Ringo? As I have already written, the arguments will continue, but they will not spoil a wonderful moment in musical history.

2012 was bringing The Hurricanes back into the limelight, and this trend was continued in September of that year when a tribute day was held for Rory at Fort Perch Rock in New Brighton. Many faces from the Merseybeat scene came together to remember Rory on the fortieth anniversary of his death. Walter Eymond (Lou Walters) was present with his family, while ex- Hurricanes' Jimmy Tushingham and Vince Earl were also in attendance. Vince played a few numbers with his band The Attractions to bring the rocking days back to the Mersey shore. Johnny Guitar's widow Margaret accepted a posthumous award that inducted

Above: Ty and Rory – two guys who left us far too early. (Courtesy of Iris Caldwell)

Right: The photo that for me sums up Rory. Sitting on a horse singing in Spain, ever ready to take the opportunity to perform, always the showman. (Courtesy of Iris Caldwell)

him into the Merseybeat Hall of Fame. A very moving and touching moment occurred when Rory's sister Iris took up the microphone to tell a number of stories about her brother while a slideshow accompanied her talk, a lovely tribute from the Merseybeat people, who never forget one of their own.

In 2015 Ringo released his album 'Postcards From Paradise', of which the first song on the album is titled 'Rory And The Hurricanes', a nice touch from Ringo to remember his old friends and former bandmates. Perhaps the biggest tribute to the group comes from those who knew them as friends and fellow musicians, who still speak fondly of the rocking band with the crazy singer. Almost fifty years since they last played together, The Hurricanes are still recalled on Merseyside by those who knew them or saw them perform. So many people describe them as nice guys, good guys, and fun guys, and that says everything after all the years that have passed. The Hurricanes remain part of musical history and always will.

10

John Byrne Talks

Bob Hardy was a good friend of John Byrne, and he has kindly allowed an interview that he made with him shortly before his death to be reproduced in this book. John had often called Bob by his middle name, Alan, in the early days, as you will notice this during the interview, which is a fascinating and moving chat with a Merseybeat legend. This is the work of Bob Hardy and, along with the photograph and postcard produced, remains copyright of Bob Hardy.

Johnny 'Guitar' Byrne talks to Bob Hardy:

I was born in Withnell Road, Old Swan, in the road almost opposite Rory Storm's house on Broad Green Road. Johnny Byrne lived just around the corner, and when I first became interested in playing myself, in 1957, you could say he was my first real 'guitar hero'. Rory's family and my family grew up together (my mum went to school with his mum, Vi Caldwell) and I saw a great deal of 'Ma Storm' during my mid-to-late teenage years, and even now I can still remember her well.

In the mid-'90s I decided to do a book of interviews with some of the Liverpool musicians I had known in the late '50s and early '60s (lucky for me I kept the interview audiotapes). I started interviewing John in May of 1999 when he had just started complaining of numbness and lack of mobility in his shoulder. He told me he thought he had caught something from a bleeding accident victim he had come into contact with during his job as a Paramedic. Unfortunately, his condition quickly got very much worse and he died four months later on 18 August 1999.

I saw him at his home the day before he died, although he was clearly very tired and not well. The hospital had sent him home, and had even lent him a special bed. I had no idea he would be dead just a few hours later; in fact I was on a flight out of the UK when it happened and I only found out about it when I got home – too late for his funeral.

John: I've done about nine interviews over the past couple of months. And, I won't do them now unless it's for people I know, or maybe the BBC or somebody like that. I'm only doing this one with you because I've known you from the early days.

Bob: Thanks John, but I should tell you that hopefully this interview will be different from the others. I think I knew you in the late '40s.

John: But you were a couple of years younger than me.

Bob: That's right! Actually I am probably the same age as your younger brother, Paul.

John: And in those days, a few years age difference in your middle-to-late teens was a big barrier.

Bob: Yes. For me at least, this is something that I believe is crucial to the understanding of what went on in the late '50s. In 1957 I was fourteen years old, and I was just too young to be involved in playing in a Skiffle group like The Texans.

John: To understand the late '50s and '60s like you, you have to have been there. At that time, a couple of years age gap made a very big difference to who you hung round with. It doesn't seem to make anything like the same difference now. In fact, ten years doesn't seem to make any difference!

Bob: Well, look at that photo of us two in 'Rushworths' in the late '50s. Spot the kid! You look cool, and I look like I've just fallen off a moped!

John: I've still got that leather jacket. Six of them were bought from a clothes shop on the Reeperbahn. The Beatles bought four, and me and Rory bought one each.

Bob: And you always looked cool John! And, there goes another Beatles story! About this interview, I've become more and more pissed off with the way the history of the sixties groups in Liverpool has been written about because it seemed like a very 'selective' and idealised view. I'll give you an example of what I mean. If there was anyone in the Beatles, the Fab four version, who was able to handle themselves and wasn't scared of a fight, it had to be George Harrison. I hung round with him at school and he was quite handy there. I was the one who used to take him up regularly to Rory's house. George had a bit of bother with one of the lads from the Swan over a girl who was Iris's friend, and he went down to look for him. For the other three, I just don't believe street fighting was ever on

Bob Hardy with Johnny 'Guitar' Byrne at Rushworths.

the agenda, and to me the whole 'working-class hero' bit is a bit suspect, and also the fact they are written about as if they were the only ones to come back to Liverpool from Hamburg with leather jackets.

John: Well, in the case of Ringo, there's even the fact that in the beginning he didn't want to be a drummer. It was only when we got the contract for Butlins in 1958 after auditioning at the Grafton. The pay was £5 a week, which was a fortune in those days. Ringo said, 'I don't know if I want to go', because he had an apprenticeship. I think he made children's climbing frames and those sorts of things in Speke, something like that. In those days, most drummers in Skiffle groups didn't even have a kit. I think Ringo had a snare drum, a tom-tom, and a cymbal. Rory said, 'We'll get the rest of the kit for you between us, and take it out of your wages.' Ringo's parents weren't very happy because being an apprentice then was what everyone wanted to do. Except for me, I think I got sacked from every job that I was in.

Bob: I remember you and Rory working in town at this time. I used to get the number 6 or 40 tram into town to get to school at the Liverpool

Institute, and I hated it, so I was nearly always late. Rory would often get the same tram to work, and he hated that. We used to talk, or rather, he would tell me what was going on, and I would listen. We must have been late nearly every day.

John: Rory worked in a firm above me in the Cotton Exchange. I think it was a called 'Bungie and Company?' I was always on time, but I still got the sack though! Paul McCartney's dad used to work above me, and he used to come down to talk to me. I was what they used to call an invoice clerk, and I'd be sitting at this machine which looked like an abacus, pushing these levers and it working out the net of a load of cotton for some ship. Anyway, Paul's dad used to come in and see me and tell me about Paul being in a group because it was reasonably well-known that me and Rory were in the Texans. He'd say, 'They're gonna be good,' and I'd say, 'Oh yeah!' because at that time they were still the Quarrymen, and they were pretty hopeless!

Bob: Where were your gigs at this time?

John: Anything we could get hold of, including auditions. We always used to try and get auditions that would pay your bus fare. Bear in mind that very few people in those days had a car, particularly young people. I would just jump on the bus with this Spanish guitar. There was one advertised in the daily papers, I think it was £8; it looked as if it had been made out of an orange box. I think John Lennon sent for one at the same time as me? You could buy guitars in music shops, or what they called music shops in the fifties, but I sent off for mine. And, this thing arrived in a cardboard box, with the most hideous sunburst, a six-string acoustic with a hole in the middle which you could just about tune and play E, A, and B7. It didn't have any scratch-board, and I can remember going to a place in Paradise Street that sold melamine and plastic and buying a square foot. I remember drawing the shape of a scratch-board and gluing it onto the guitar. A guy who used to get us a lot of bookings at that time is in *Brookside* now, that's Al T. Cossey-Alan Cosgrove. He lived in Old Swan as well, Leinster Road, and he always seemed old to me. In fact, he still looks exactly the same to me now, although we both went to St Oswald's school at about the same time. He was a Club Comic and he used to get us bookings on, say, Moreton Labour Club, for fifteen shillings (75p). Now, as you know, Moreton's a long way. You used to have to get the train, and then we had to walk from the station to the club carrying all the gear. Al T. Cossey would get 10 per cent. He was a bit of an agent I suppose.

Bob: Who was in 'The Texans' at this time?

John: There was Rory, me, John Carter who lived near the 'Rocket' on rhythm. We had 'Spud' Ward, who used to play with the 'Merseysippi', on slap bass. The fellow on the washboard was Geoff Truman, who used to go to St Oswald's with me. He was a bit of a hard case from Old Swan. I think he said, 'I'll play the washboard' and we didn't argue!

Bob: Can you remember why you started to play?

John: I started in 1957. My elder brother Pat used to buy 78 records. He was a modern jazz fan, and he used to buy things like Gerry Mulligan, Stan Kenton, and Johnny Dankworth. If you listen to that stuff now, it's still superb. And, he would also bring home Elvis 78s, and he also bought the Lonnie Donegan Decca 78, 'Rock Island Line'. When I heard this, I really liked it, it really drove along. And, then when I saw Donegan on the TV I thought 'I could do that', but I had no guitar!

Bob: How did you learn to play a bit in the beginning?

John: Do you remember Allen Thompson in Glen Road?

Bob: Yes! He lived a couple of houses up on the left.

John: Well he had a group called The Rhythm Quartet. They used to play tunes like 'My Funny Valentine'. He taught me. He used to come down to our house and show me stuff, which didn't go down too well with my mum. He had a 'Hofner President', and he would teach me all kinds of tunes like 'My Funny Valentine'. He would write the chords down for me, and I would practice them in my bedroom for hours. I've still got the chord book. I would try and learn them, but some of the keys, like B minor, were too hard for me then. I was quite happy with three chords. So after Rory had mastered a repertoire of, 'Maggie May', 'Rock Island Line', and 'Don't You rock Me Daddy-O' things we all did, we were up and running! You'll never learn playing in your bedroom. You're better out there playing with other people. You pick things up then. It's the difference between wanting to be a guitarist and being a guitar-player. I was a guitar player; I just wanted to play the stuff I was interested in. I have never been interested in playing the guitar for the sake of it.

Bob: I can remember you copying licks of an Everly Brothers Album, one afternoon when I was round at your house.

John: Yes, that was in 1957. It was the one with the two of them on motorbikes. Later, when Wally joined the Hurricanes we did 'Brand New Heartache' from that album.

Bob: I remember him doing it, he had a great voice and it was his party piece for the Hurricanes. Was there much mixing with the early groups at that time?

John: Well, Rory Storm and The Hurricanes were the only group that mixed with The Beatles for long periods of time. There was only one rhythm guitar player at that time who was as good as me and that was John Lennon.

Bob: I remember at the time, he admired your right-hand guitar technique.

John: I was much faster, but he was a real good hard, powerful, player. So, I liked his style, and he liked mine. We were with them for months in Hamburg, and we lived with them. I'm not talking here about the odd gig on the Orrell Park Ballroom, or the Tower, this was in Hamburg at the Kaiserkeller, the club I nicked the posters from that are in all the books. It was a dangerous place, the Reeperbahn. I'm not talking about the Star Club, which was a sanitised gig, no real danger there if you know what I mean.

Bob: Yes I played there in 1966 and it was just like a normal well-run club. But I remember the Beatles at the Top Ten on the Reeperbahn well because I stayed there with them for a few nights in 1961 when the ship I was on dry-docked there for nine days, when I was a 'Sparks' in the Merchant Navy. The club was OK, and although there's been all kinds of stuff written about the accommodation being crap, I can't say I remember too much about staying there overnight because I was so pissed. But George seemed made up to see me, and it was him who offered to let me stay upstairs with the band. I used Paul's bunk. I seem to remember he was staying with some girl on a houseboat or something. Of course I had no idea they were going to be so big. At the time I was too knocked out with seeing and talking to Tony Sheridan for one thing.

John: I knew then that they were going to be big. I knew them when they were the Quarrymen, and they played at that place we had called The Morgue in 1958. Remember?

Bob: I remember bringing George Harrison round from school to go to The Morgue. Going there was the high point of my life at that time. I remember it was in a nurses' home at the back of Oakhill Park in Broad Green.

John: That's right; it was in a detached house in its own grounds, with a driveway up to the front door. To the right of the house was 'Sibron's

Postcard from Hamburg that John sent to Bob.

Field', a patch of land with just the concrete foundations of a house on it, and we all used to play on it when we were kids.

Bob: Yeah! We used to cook chips on it!

John: I always remember me and Rory found this horse's head there, and all you younger ones like you were going round there for weeks just to look at it. How it got there I'll never know. To the left of the house was more houses. You had to go round the back to the entrance of The Morgue. Into the kitchen and then down the stairs into the cellars, it was there. It was a long rectangular room, with a stage about 6 inches off the ground.

Bob: Did The Morgue predate the Casbah?

John: Yes, it did predate the Casbah, because when we were doing the Casbah thing, in 1957, I used to keep a proper diary. I couldn't keep one now to save my life. This is a poster of the Buddy Holly gig at the Philharmonic on the 20 March 1958. Now I would have given the earth to see Buddy Holly, but I couldn't go because that was the date that we opened The Morgue. And, remember, The Quarrymen were on for the first gig, with George Harrison doing an audition for them. I remember saying to Rory there was no ventilation, so I bought a 'Vent-Axia' fan to try and get some air in. The room was lit with red light bulbs. George Harrison wanted to join our group first, and came to Rory's with you, but Vi wouldn't let you in because we were practising under the stairs at the time. We didn't know anything about it, but she thought he was too young. We could have done with another guitar player. We ended up getting Ty. When The Morgue closed down, I walked the 4 1/2 miles to the Casbah to ask Mrs Best if she wanted to book us. But she said she already had a band, and that was the Quarrymen, with Pete. But she hired Rory a lot later on; in fact I'm surprised at the number of times we did play there.

Bob: Can you remember who played at The Morgue?

John: Yes. The Quarrymen played, the Bluejeans, and Paul Rogers (Paul Murphy). I made a recording with Paul Murphy in Phillip's studio in Kensington, this was in 1957. We did the Little Richard tune 'She's got It' and 'Butterfly', the Charlie Gracie tune. I reckon that's what gave The Beatles the idea to record. The reason I had the recording was that Paul Murphy had no money – I know you'll find that hard to believe – and he asked me to buy it. I think it was about five bob. He was the first one of that generation to make a real record, 'Four And Twenty Thousand Kisses', on HMV.

Bob: I remember that! My sister bought it. How did The Morgue start?

John: Mrs Thompson, who owned the house used to rent out rooms to nurses and university students. So, we got them to talk her into letting us use the cellar.

Bob: I remember there were complaints to the police, and trouble from the neighbours. How long did it last?

John: Only a couple of months. The police closed it down. The couple next door, Mr and Mrs Brown, would get incensed with all the 'goings-on' in the front garden. Couples rolling about on the lawn! But, as I say, the police eventually closed it, and we could never find another place.

Bob: The room was still there in 1964. I had started playing in a band called 'TL's Bluesicians' and I went to see Mrs Thompson. She let us use the cellar that The Morgue was in to practice. It looked exactly the same!

John: Yes she was great. She was way ahead of her time. When she let us use that cellar we could only have been about seventeen at the time.

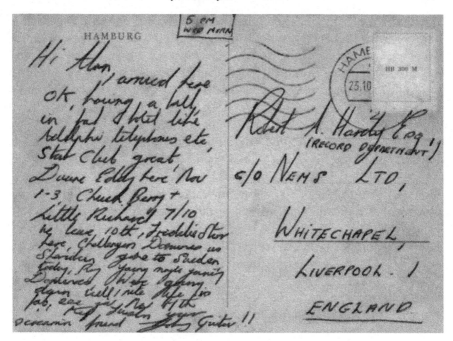

Reverse of the postcard that John sent to Bob.

I remember that Johnny Ball, Zoe Ball's father, used to live there. He was a Bluecoat at Pwllheli, and then he became a Redcoat. He was a drummer, and had a red premier drum kit. He was eccentric by today's standards even then. Later on he moved into Rory's house.

Bob: Yeah I used to talk to him a lot when he lived there. Another one who became famous! When did you start the move away from Skiffle?

John: In 1958 we were on the Empire and won the heat of the Skiffle competition, which included a free holiday at Butlin's, Pwllheli. We started doing Rock 'n' Roll then.

Bob: Can you remember any of the other Skiffle groups at that time? Was Faron or Carl Terry about yet?

John: No, they were younger than us, and they'd only just be getting started. The groups about were 'The Darktown Skiffle Group', the 'Clayton' Skiffle group with Ringo, 'The Brian Newman Skiffle Group', he was coloured and very good, 'The Bluejeans', and 'The Gin-Mill Skiffle Group'. A little while later the whole thing just boomed. That would be when you got into it.

Bob: Yeah. I did my first gig on the Regent Cinema, a Saturday-morning matinee, with Phil Perry from Glen Road. I think Gabby Gore and Wally Shepherd had already done it with what must have been the members of the TT's with Lance Railton. I had a steel Dobro, it had like blue enamel on it and one of the sound-cones was dodgy. It must have been around 1959.

John: You got that guitar off Mrs Jobson in Whitehouse Road. Jackie Jobson, one of the sons, was a good friend of mine.

Bob: That's right. I used to collect American comics, and so did they, so we'd swap. I remember you were into them at that time as well.

John: That's right, I used to collect the old E. C. horror comics like *Tales From The Crypt*. They were banned by the government for a long time.

Bob: Speaking of guitars, did you still have the cheap Spanish one when you went to Butlins, or had you moved on?

John: Rory had a Hofner Senator; I'd changed mine to an Aristone. You came down to the Blue Ball with me in Prescot Street when I tried to sell it. It was in the window for weeks; I think the shop had it there for £5. I wish I hadn't sold it now as it's the only one I ever saw. It was an electric.

Bob: What was the story on that Antoria of yours?

John: After I put the 'Aristone' up for sale I went to Rushworths and saw this weird looking thing. It was the Antoria, it was £32 I think. This was about 1958. I just liked the weird shape. And, do you know it has been photographed everywhere. I liked it, but I didn't have enough money to buy it. We were still a Skiffle group, 'The Texans', but we knew that Rock 'n' Roll was coming in. The Antoria was a solid, and it looked the part, unlike the cello shape of the Aristone. Anyway, I asked my dad to sign for the HP. At first he told me I should forget the guitar and get a proper job, but after a lot of 'umming and aahing' he eventually signed for it. I've still got all the documents. There was a problem though because if you have a solid body electric guitar, then you must have an amplifier! Nobody had one in those days; there were none in the shops. Nobody had ever seen a Fender even. So Paul Murphy had this thing made up. One of the speakers came from the Hippodrome cinema in West Derby Road. It had been used for the first talkie, *The Jazz Singer*. There was one speaker on each side of the cinema in front of the screen, and one of those speakers was now mine! Inside the home-made case was a little valve amplifier, and to make it look smart I cut a bolt of lightning out of plywood and stuck it on the front of the speaker. Murphy photographed me in St Luke's hall and I've got my sunglasses on top of it, my 'set list'. You could have had a tea set on the top! It had a bit of a plastic handle, and if there was no P.A. or bass-amp then two of us would plug into this thing. It must have had an output of 10 to 15 watts, but it worked, and I used it for ages. I used to hump it round on the bus; I'd put it under the stairs on those old double-deckers.

Bob: So you were playing Rock 'n' Roll by now?

John: Yes.

Bob: Well, here's a question I've always wanted to ask you. I remember that the group was barred from the Cavern in the early days for playing a Rock 'n' Roll song.

John: Yes that's right! Ray McFall fined us, and said that if we wanted to play on the Cavern again, we weren't to play Rock 'n' Roll. We did 'Whole Lotta Shakin Goin On'.

Bob: Do you remember the night I played with you on the Cavern? Ringo was engaged to some girl called Maureen or Margaret (I think she was a hairdresser or something like that) and he couldn't do the second set?

John: Yeah I do!

The Hurricanes at The Cavern. You can see Johnny's amp with the bolt of lightning on it. (Courtesy of Walter Eymond)

Bob: I have this picture in my head of you turning round to me at the beginning of a number, I think it was Marty Wilde's 'Endless Sleep', and saying, 'Don't worry, it's easy!' I'd never played the drums in my life! Hey! I suppose I could actually say that I sat in for Ringo Starr!

John: Yeah, you could say that. We were the very first band in Liverpool to play Rock 'n' Roll at the Cavern. Everyone was booing, and the beatniks threw the old big pennies at us. In the end I went round and picked them all up. We were getting £10 and I think we got fined £3. I knew Rock 'n' Roll would soon replace Skiffle because when we were at Butlins on the holiday that we won at the Empire, I saw a Rock 'n' Roll band called Rory Blackwell and the Blackjacks. They got sacked from Butlins, and Rory Blackwell came to me, and asked me to join his band there and then. He was going to do a theatre nearby, and he only had three of his band left. So I started playing with him on this theatre, doing stuff like, 'Brand New Cadillac', and 'Something Else'. He wanted me to go to London with him, but Rory said, 'We're gonna be bigger than them', and we were childhood friends, so at the end of the week I told Blackwell I wouldn't do it. So, he took another guy on who was at the holiday camp who played piano, a woolly-back from Leigh. His name was Clive Powell, but he changed it later on to Georgie Fame. So, I went back to Liverpool with Rory Storm. Skiffle was on the way out, and we were all listening seriously to Rock 'n' Roll. I can remember you bringing that Johnny Burnette record 'Honey Hush' to our house and sitting at my mum's dining table while I worked out the solo for you. Nobody knew what it was at that time. I loved James Burton, but I could never play like him, and anyway, I was a rhythm guitarist.

I remember that Britain was getting Rock 'n' Roll shows over from America, and Allan Williams said that he was going to put Gene Vincent and Eddie Cochran on the Boxing stadium, together with local groups Gerry and the Pacemakers, Rory Storm and the Hurricanes, and Cass and the Cassanovas. So, we were made up! A week before the show Eddie Cochran died and Allan had to put new flyers out. We did the show and Rory was a knockout. The Beatles wanted to do it, but Allan Williams didn't think that they were good enough, but they were in the audience. The place was jammed.

I used to get any hand-outs with my name on it. First, there was 'The Texans Skiffle Group', and then it was 'Al Caldwell and the Texans Skiffle Group'. Then, 'Al Storm', then 'Jet Storm', then finally 'Rory Storm'. When we got to do the Stadium, I cut out all the photos. There was a black singer on called Davy Jones. I asked him for his autograph and he gave me the pen he was using – it was a Parker. Not only that, he gave me the Parker pencil with it! I've still got them. I always remember that. I collected every dance poster, everything. In the Kaiserkeller, Rory and

I took one of the posters each. I have kept them all these years, every flyer and every poster. I have the biggest collection of Liverpool memorabilia; I've sold five posters for £15,000 and I've still got seventy. I sold the Kaiserkeller one for £3,800. It's at the Hardrock Café now.

Bob: Can you say something about the time Ringo left to join the Beatles.

John: Ringo left us in '62, and when they got 'Love Me Do' into the charts it caused a sensation in Liverpool; it was unheard of. But when the Beatles started touring with people like Helen Shapiro, I always thought it would have been nice if they could have given us a job at the bottom of the bill. We weren't as good as them musically, but Rory was a still a better performer. But Rory and me had a great lifestyle anyway, and we owned our own cars before any of them.

Bob: I remember Ringo had a big Ford at the time. I used to go out with him driving at night. He loved it.

John: I went with him to Whitney's in Scotland Road for that car, and the fella there was trying to get us out. I think we were both dressed in black. Anyway, Ringo looks at this Ford cream-and-blue Zodiac.

Bob: That was it!!

John: And it was really Americanized, it was brilliant. We called the fellow over and Ringo said, 'We'll take that!' And he couldn't believe it! Ringo fished in his pocket and brought out the money there and then. I think this was 1960 and the car was 450–500 pounds, which was a lot of money then. Anyway, we walked out because they were going to service it, and Ringo went back and picked it up the next day.

At this point we finished the interview, and regrettably, although John helped clean up this part, we didn't do any more taping, although we did a great more talking.

© Bob Hardy, 1999

11

Hurricanes Memories

Walter Eymond (Lou Walters): 'I am reluctant to give interviews anymore as it is very annoying talking to authors only for them to go away and write whatever they want to. The books are filled with so many untruths and are written for sales not facts. I had no interest in being interviewed for this book until I was convinced of its true direction.

Being a member of the band was a wonderful and fantastic experience that took me to many places. It was fun, so much fun, though we had our moments where we could have gladly punched one another's lights out. We were all close friends. I had played as a kid with Charlie (Ty) around the Old Swan area long before we both joined the band. We had grown up together, practised our music together, had a whole lot of laughs together, and when the need arose, stood and fought together. Charlie was my best friend. Johnny was the smooth dude who would almost slide onto a stage with his coolness, and then Rory, where do you start with Rory? Nobody was like him. He was a top-class showman. They were great guys who I miss so much. Ringo was a good lad, as were most of the drummers who played with us. Jimmy Tushingham was a top bloke who was great fun. I was heartbroken when Charlie and Rory died. When I heard of Rory's death and the suggestions of suicide I thought "No way is that True." Rory would never have done that. He loved life and lived it to the full.

I have read and heard that we did not like The Beatles, even hated their success. Again, total rubbish. We hung out with them for a long time; the guys from both bands were very close. I was very good friends with Pete Best and would go out with him a lot. We were very happy for them when they made it big. They were a very good band who I noticed were starting to adapt and change. I was pushing Rory to follow their lead, as was Charlie and Johnny. It never happened for us, but that is just the way life goes. We were a part of an incredible musical era, and they were fantastic days that I will never forget.'

Jim Skillicorn: 'It is sixty-two years since I was at school with Alan at Highfield Secondary Modern. I was in the same class as him, and Walter, his guitarist, was in the year below. My contact with Alan was as friends, who spent our lunchtimes eating chips at his house in Broad Green Road instead of buying school dinners! He showed me some photos of him as a child dressed in a drummer boy outfit when he'd been in a show, dancing and singing. He did tell me he was taught to tap dance, but I was not to tell anyone else at school. His mother was very keen on both Alan and his sister being on the stage. I think he told me she had been a dancer. Every time I saw his father he seemed to be in a tracksuit. I'm not sure what he did for a living?

At school Alan was good at sport. He played football on the wing as he was very fast and as you most probably know, he was a very good runner. He ran for a club, but I don't know which one. I think his father was involved with running? I lost contact after we left school, but after I'd done my national service in the navy I went to the Grafton one night with my wife, and as I walked in Alan came walking towards me. I said 'Hello Al' and he just walked straight past me. Later I saw Walter and when I told him what had happened he laughed and said "You can't expect him to answer you, he's Rory Storm." Having been away for some time I didn't have a clue who Rory Storm was, so you can imagine my surprise when Walter explained who Alan had become.

I have always thought it strange that Alan did not have the success of other Liverpool groups, as I think he was bigger in Liverpool than any of the others as Liverpool music became world famous.'

A guy who wants to be known as John: 'I used to go to Butlins Pwllheli in the '50s with mom and dad. Mom was a musician and I a singer, and they had talent competitions where free holidays could be won, which we managed to do three years running. We went to watch Rory Storm and The Hurricanes on many occasions and I'm pretty sure my mum met his mum in the audience. I was very young, but I do recall my dad moaning about their drummer practising his drums in his chalet in the afternoon when dad was trying to have a nap. The comment I remember was, "I wish that big-nose bugger would stop practising his drums so I can get some sleep." I leave it to you to guess who he was referring to. There is another time when I remember the girls on the front row were screaming their heads off at Rory, which did not go down well with the boyfriends, and so Rory had to do a runner after the show, which involved crossing a railway track.'

Ann Blakely: 'I only really remember Iris and she was about four/five years older than me. I can remember her mother and their house that was

The lads at The Cavern. (Courtesy of Iris Caldwell)

across the road from Winnie Mac's. All I can really remember is that Iris was really attractive, and together with another girl called Ann they used to play the parts of principal girl and boy in panto at the David Lewis – Iris would be Prince Charming or Dandini.'

Carl Wharton, who has performed as Rory Storm on many occasions: 'After first hearing about Rory in the late '80s I knew that one day I would portray him on stage. Straight away I felt a spiritual connection with him, and I had no reservations in speaking to him to ask for any help. The role presented many challenges such as singing as a frontman, pushing energy levels to the max with leaps and bounds, but the biggest challenge would be presenting my portrayal to Iris, Johnny Guitar and all those that knew and loved Rory. It gave me the opportunity to know a man that sadly I couldn't meet in person. To date it has been the most rewarding experience that I have presented on stage. Thanks Rory.'

Kathleen Faulkner: 'I was just a kid, and it was a great time to be young, but we never thought about it. I loved Rory because he was so nice, a lot nicer than most of the bands. He would come into the Black Cat club after his gig, stand in the corner watching whoever was on – very shy, always polite. I met my husband Les in the Black Cat by then, and we stopped going to the mad places. I saw them a lot at the Aintree Inny; it was friendlier in there, and more local. I was married and living in Haydock when Rory died. One of my sisters rang to tell me. I was heartbroken. He was just not in the right place at the right time. They were one of so many; they would go missing and pop up again. It was only years later that I knew they were going to Germany.

I knew a band in the Black cat with Hank Walters as a member. I think Rory knew him well because I remember him going to a party up Netherfield Road with Hank. We were asked to go, but didn't. Many years later, when we were home in Liverpool, I saw in the *Echo* that Hank was playing in a pub along the dock road, so me and Les went along. When he had a break we went over and told him who we were. He did not know us, but he announced it over the mike: "This couple knew me in 1963." Everyone clapped and made a big fuss of us, and we talked about old times. We sat with his daughters, and I kept shouting out old songs he used to sing and he shouted back, "Blimey girl How old are yer?" We had a great night just laughing about all the bands and where they were now – of course Rory had died by then. Rory Storm and The Hurricanes were just as good, if not better, than the Beatles in my opinion, and they did 'Long Tall Sally' better than anyone else. The Beatles were one of many many bands, and nobody thought one was better than the others. Ian and the Zodiacs, The Big Three, Gerry and The Pacemakers; what talent we had in our city.'

Geoff Riley: 'The Hurricanes, along with The Big Three and Kingsize Taylor and The Dominoes, were one of the best bands in Liverpool. I never rated The Beatles very much, and I still never did until their recordings from 1967 onwards. The Hurricanes had a fantastic show; you could feel the buzz of the people watching them perform. Rory was brilliant on stage. Nobody else was like him; he mesmerised you, you just had to watch him.'

Arty Davies: 'At one concert at Bankfield House youth club, Garston, Liverpool, in 1965, my band The Pressure Points supported Rory Storm and the Hurricanes. The stage lighting failed between sets. Storm was upset until Mr Taylor walked in with a massive flashlight and he turned to me: "Here, you might be the best to do this, use this as a spotlight on Rory." I was sweating and knackered trying to keep up with Rory Storm. Anybody who has seen Rory perform would understand why. At the

The Hurricanes with drummer Brian Johnson. Johnny looks asleep, and we have a rare glimpse of Lou without his glasses. (Courtesy of Iris Caldwell)

end of the night I was leaving to walk home and Johnny Guitar came up and said "Blimey you did well, where do you live?" I said basically just around the corner, and Johnny said get in I will give you a lift, so I jumped into Johnny's Jag and got a lift home.

Mick Shields: 'I saw The Hurricanes play at The New Brighton open-air Pavilion, The Orrell Park Ballroom (OPB), and The Aintree Institute. I only spoke to Rory once. I'm a Blue and he was a Red, so a bit of banter went on though we only had a few words. On stage Rory's energy was amazing and he was always so smartly dressed. Everyone would be dancing away when the group played. They are my all-time favourite band.

Tommy Moore, ex-Beatles drummer, talking to the author in 1978: 'I saw the Hurricanes play a number of times. They were a great band with a real thumping sound. Rory Storm – what can you say? – fantastic performer. I sat in with them a couple of times; us drummers were lucky like that as we were in short supply and got to sit in with a lot of the groups. They were all nice lads, very down to earth and no cockiness about them. Rory was a charming bloke, you could not help but like him, and there was not a bad bone in his body. Rory, along with George Harrison, are two of the nicest human beings I have ever had the pleasure to meet.'

Angela Fitzpatrick: 'I worked with John Byrne in the ambulance service in the late '80s/early '90s, working out of Crosby ambulance station. He was just a great guy, always up for a laugh and had some fab stories that he would share. He was also a very committed and caring ambulance man, or emergency medical technician as they're known now. You knew if you were teamed up with John you had a mate you could rely on, whom would always watch your back and who always put the patients as a priority. There are no specific stories that I can recall other than he was more than happy to show colleagues his vast collection of records and memorabilia that he had collected over the years. He made me some mixed cassette tapes of Rock 'n' Roll and some rare songs that I still have. He always looked like a rock star, always had his hair just so, and when he was on his way to or from work he always wore a leather jacket. He drove a Scimitar too, and he just always looked like a real cool dude. He loved life and was taken long before his time. He is very sadly missed.'

Janet Dean: 'Me and a friend would go along to watch many of the bands. We were only fourteen when we started going and were terrified of being thrown out, but it was so exciting, the Liverpool bands were great. We would get ourselves into a small corner so as not to be spotted then run for the bus home. The first time I saw Rory Storm and The Hurricanes I was stunned, blown away; they were fantastic and Rory was bouncing everywhere across the stage. You just could not take your eyes off them. Then, Rory spotted us and kept looking over; we felt all grown up with the handsome singer staring at us. When the band took a break, Rory came straight to us, picked up our glasses of coke and took a sip of each, before telling us "Do not let me catch you drinking alcohol." He asked us how old we were, and after we had fibbed to him he made us tell him for real. He told us he would make sure we got home OK. After they had finished their show he sent over Johnny Guitar, who put us in his car and drove us home while the others packed away their gear. Any time that Rory saw us after that night he would say "It better be coke you're drinking." He was so nice, as were all of the band. Looking back, I can see that he was just taking care of two young girls. I will always remember his kindness, and that of Johnny. They were a very special bunch of lads in that band, always happy to talk with people, always smiling.'

Ted 'Kingsize' Taylor: 'Rory's followers were made up of mostly girls – perhaps this was because of his effeminate attitude during his performances,

A suntanned Johnny and Rory with a couple of Hurricanettes. Eileen is sitting with Johnny. (Courtesy of Iris Caldwell)

very 'I love me', 'who do you love', which they could relate to themselves in those days. (This does not mean that he was effeminate when off-stage.) The band was only just better than the average bunch of lads, trying hard to improve their musical skills while having a lot of fun. Don't forget, none of us ever thought that we would ever become professionals at that time. Band members were chopping and changing, and some bands created heavier versions of the new phenomenon called Rock 'n' Roll, predicted as being dead in a couple of years. This did not happen and the whole situation turned around, and bands became of more appeal to the hairy-arsed working-class lads on Merseyside who loved the loud pumping sound which they could dance around to, mostly on their own or in gangs, all doing their own thing. But Rory was still quite happy with what he was doing and stuck to it. In spite of that, he just loved what he loved doing best, and that's what it's all about. Love what you Love. He was always a bit of a loner, and a very insecure person, but he always said that he liked me, maybe because I had no hang-ups about disabilities or impediments. This was because two of our family had speech impediments also. It was me that told him to sing his speech (A tip from my Aunty Dot) and that did help him a lot. I liked him as a person and as a performer. I was mortified when I heard about his death. We all were. RIP Rory.'

David Owens: 'My memories of Rory and the Hurricanes were when they played at the "Jive Hive" St Lukes Hall, Crosby, one of my regular haunts. They would always attract a good following, especially females, so it naturally followed the boys would be thinking a much better and larger selection of girls to choose from. It was a unique dance hall in that it had a wooden sprung floor affair; with a concentrated effort of all the dancers you could exaggerate the spring motion. The beat timing of the bands performing would assist the boppers moving in unison to get it really bouncing. Many of the groups had a dedicated following of fans who would travel around the many dance halls. Rory was high in this pecking order; it could also lead to a bit of aggravation when it was lads involved, coming onto the local manor so as to speak, to accompany girlfriends.

When Rory performed he didn't just front a group of musicians and belt out the latest in what was being broadcast from among the top ten records, as many groups of the era seemed to think was the deal. With Rory you got a stage show as well, with songs from the musical shows. He was always prancing across the stage; being a well-tuned athlete he was able to go that bit further in what he did as well. So, you got in addition, a good level of theatre performance from him. The band also took a lead from what the "Shadows" did, with them also adding in some choreographed footwork. His flamboyant style, as he became more popular, transcended into the stage suits and costumes for himself and the band. (Maybe if it were today he would have been destined for the musical theatre.) His long blonde hair and slim tall 6-foot physique made him into an idol of the females. This unfortunately led to the girls, when he performed, just gathering in front of the stage screeching and encouraging him to go that bit further with his showboating, which he lapped up and often went on his knee to sing softly to these stage-front fans. He also obliged them with his exaggerated hair combing act. I am sure it was a trick he borrowed from the character Kookie from the TV series *77 Sunset Strip*.

This action of the females gathering in front of the stage was a bit of a bummer for the lads having paid money to get into the dance hall – a sore point and at times very frustrating as they watched all this adulation while not getting a look in, nor a chance to chat up or dance with the girls. There was no alcohol served in the Jive Hive, notwithstanding you could get a 'pass out' to go across to the Crosby Hotel for a few pints of 'Dutch courage'. Inevitably sometimes this became enough courage to enable the frustrated to shout out disrespectfully at the blonde performer! On occasions pennies were also thrown at him. This he took in his stride, collecting them up and thanking the missile throwers with a thumbs up and a big smile. Some dance halls were notorious for fights, usually over a girl giving more than one lad the feeling he was in with a shout. The Jive Hive was not in this category. Also, Rory was the guy in with a shout every time as far as the girls were concerned.'

Sheila Shanley: 'I had the privilege of seeing Rory Storm and the Hurricanes. One night in 1964 at the Savoy Dance Hall, Bath Street, Waterloo, Rory jumped off the stage and sat beside me singing and looking into my eyes! Fond memories. I can't even remember what song it was! I do recall him singing one song called "America" that night; I think it is from *West Side Story*? They were brilliant performers. I don't suppose we realised how great they were. I do know that I wasn't all that interested in going to see the Beatles live on stage, but a lot of people my age were of the opinion that Rory and his band were far better. I can't recall any of the other groups who played at the Savoy – Rory and his Hurricanes seemed to stand out.'

Thomas Marshall: 'I attended John Hamilton Annex, Carisbrooke Road, and went to Queens Drive Baths. This would be around 1965. I have only recently lost the medallion that I received while there. My instructor was Rory Storm, a lean blonde guy, quite helpful, and good at explaining what was needed. I had a lot of respect for him.'

Jean Beach (nee Kelly): 'I grew up in Broad Green Road and was friends with Iris Caldwell. Her brother Alan was such a lovely person. He and Johnny Byrne were originally a Skiffle group, and it was amazing that when he sang there was no sign of the stammer. Alan was a bit of an extrovert, but he was not offensive to anyone, he was just being himself. I can recall him running for the Harriers. When he had a road race Mrs Caldwell would make flags and banners for all us kids, and we would line up on the road to cheer him on. When he came running past we would all be waving and shouting "Come on Alan". My mum and Mrs Caldwell were great friends and they could relate to each other. After she had been to dance class, Iris would rehearse with her mother at home; she practised every day and was such a talent. Mr Caldwell was a Porter at Broadgreen hospital, and he used to ride a bike and collect newspapers. He was such a lovely person.

The Caldwell's used to have a long shed on the path, and we would host our Halloween shows there for bonfire night. The money we collected went towards fireworks and potatoes for the bonfires that we had in my back garden. On several occasions Alan would hide dressed in a sheet, pretending to be a ghost. He would sit at the back of the shed, and the little horror would scare us and send us off screaming. They had a dog called Toby, who used to lick the sores on your legs if you let him.

I can remember the band used to rehearse in the back garden of Alan's home. We would run around to 'Sibron's Field' in Oakhill Park and listen to them. Alan was once banned from local radio after he said the word 'virgin' on air – things were a lot more strict back then. The Liverpool bands, including The Hurricanes, were so so important, and are a part of history. The Beatles tend to get all of the mentions, and some people do not really seem to want to hear about the other bands that helped put them on the map. Alan was so devastated when Ringo left the band, they were both so close. He was never the same after it.

The last time that I spoke to Alan, and saw him, he was coming down the stairs of his home wearing a tiny pair of Speedo swimming trunks. He was beautiful, an amazing person and a great talent. I remember the funeral of Alan and Mrs Caldwell, with the coffins being carried side by side. As Alan supported Liverpool, they played "When you Walk through a Storm". It really affected me so much as I had known them since my cradle days. It truly was so very sad, and I do still think of them.'

Alice Connor: 'I knew Charles O'Brien very well as we had both lived in the same street – Pemberton Road. He used to play with us kids in the road and we called him Chas. He was a bit quiet, but a nice lad all the same. As he got older he took up dancing and boxing, and was very good at both; I remember seeing the trophies in his house. He also played guitar, and was a bit of a local celebrity when he joined the Hurricanes. He was very good looking, not that I fancied him; he was just my old mate from the street. He always stopped to say hello when he saw me, even when he was in his band. It was such a shock when I heard he had

Ty and Lou backstage at the Star-Club, Hamburg, with Duane Eddy whom they billed with at the club in 1963. (Courtesy of Walter Eymond)

died, I was so upset. Life is so unfair at times, he was taken too soon. I never knew the other band members or saw them play, but I can tell you that Chas was such a lovely guy.'

Mary Leathan: 'My favourite band on the Liverpool scene was The Searchers, but I did see Rory Storm and The Hurricanes play a few times at the Peppermint Lounge on London Road. Rory was always a fabulous showman who gave his all; they were a very good group. He and the rest of the band were also very friendly, and would say "hello" or "how are you" to people in the crowd as they came off stage. I later found out that Rory lived very close to me, and that he had a sister, Iris, and was devoted to his mother.

Noel 'Noochy' Davies: 'I sang a song with the band at Butlins and won twenty cigarettes, which Rory presented to me. I met him and the Hurricanes a lot during the early '60s as we played the same venues in Merseyside and North Wales. Fabulous days; great times.

Paul Gilbert: 'They were a good band; anyone who says otherwise either never saw them or is still jealous of them. They were all top guys who you could have a laugh and joke with. I knew Wally (Lou) really well, and would chat to him whenever I saw him. They pushed the boundaries in those early days, wearing suits and doing dance routines as they played, and Rory, he would try anything to please a crowd; he was eccentric and at times brilliant. Ignore what some Beatles books tell you, the Hurricanes were a good band: Ty was a very good lead guitarist, Johnny pushed the rhythm hard, Lou had a thumping bass sound, and Ringo kept them in beat. You do not become one of the biggest bands in Liverpool and have a big following if you are no good. I enjoyed watching them as they gave a great show, plus there was no cockiness about them; they were just down to earth lads.'

Ronnie Blackwell: 'I knew Rory when he worked in Jersey in 1972. I had a friend called Pam who's boyfriend was a DJ named Sparky. Pam had a boutique with a massive flat above it. I worked in a salon around the corner called the 'house of curls' and I used to buy a lot of my clothes from Pam and do her hair – that's how we became friends – so any parties that went on I was always invited. With Sparky being a DJ, all the musicians would attend any parties, like Norman Hale from Liverpool. He was brilliant on piano, good old Rock 'n' Roll, and of course Rory.

One night we were all at a party at Pam's when Rory said to me, "Tomorrow night, you are going to be one of my backing singers." I replied " Oh Yeah" thinking he was joking. It was all hot pants and boots then and he told me to put my best outfit on as I would be on that stage. The next night he did a gig at the local cinema in St Helier; I had come along to watch and was stunned when he announced "I've got some nice young ladies to join me now", before dragging me up along with a couple of others. I was so nervous, but once I got up there it was great and I ended up dancing on a piano. Rory had a way about him that helped you feel at ease. It was a great time, all so long ago now, but everybody loved Rory.'

Author's Comments

Why Rory Storm and The Hurricanes? They were a very popular band who were among the trendsetters on the Merseyside music scene. They could rock a venue and thrill a crowd – a great band with one of the best frontmen in the business leading them. Ringo Starr was among their members, and they pushed and encouraged him to sing songs and take his own spot during gigs. They were nice guys, and are still highly spoken of today. Bigger than The Beatles? At one time they dwarfed them, with John, Paul and George looking up to them. In virtually every book that has been written about The Beatles you will find a mention of Rory Storm and The Hurricanes. After all, Ringo Starr was the drummer with the band before he became a Beatle, plus the two groups were good friends and played many shows together. So, it is easy to see why they are talked about in Beatles history. A large percentage of the Beatles books will give The Hurricanes a mere passing glance, while others regard them as just the band that Ringo played with. A few do go into more detail and give them the credit that they deserve. Sadly The Hurricanes fall into the category of Merseyside bands whose importance and talent is far too often ignored, along with the likes of Kingsize Taylor and The Dominos, Derry Wilkie and The Seniors, The Big Three, The Undertakers, and The Remo Four. Their importance in the creation of the Merseyside music scene is far more than as just the band who once had Ringo as a drummer; they were much much more than that.

I find it sad to read comments such as 'Ty Brien died and the band broke up' or 'The Hurricanes guitarist died.' Little is written about him; he was a real person and deserves to be remembered for who he was. Walter (Lou) Eymond has not disappeared off the face of the earth as some claim. What Ringo and the other ex-band members think when they read people writing that Walter is the only member of The Hurricanes still alive we can only guess – probably they laugh at it. Many guys who played with the band are still around, and many are still rocking and rolling.

I am no expert on The Hurricanes, just a very keen fan. I have interviewed many people connected to the band, and over many years I have read countless books and articles that mention them. I spent many hours researching the family trees of the guys in order to make their story more complete. I have travelled up and down the country to meet people, and flew to Hamburg to see the places where they played and stayed and to record yet more interviews. A long time was spent going through old newspapers and records from schools and churches, even listings of The Beatles gigs to check event dates. I have tried to confirm all details and stories that I have found, but a few errors will probably have made it into the book. If so, please forgive me.

Basically, I wanted the lads in the band to be remembered for whom they were, and I hope that this book has gone some small way to doing that. However, there is another reason why I wanted to pay tribute to the lads in a book, a very personal and special reason for myself.

When I was three years old a fire raged through the ground floor of my family home. I was upstairs at the time and cut off from safety by the flames. A very brave fireman risked his own life as he entered the building to save me. I do not even know his name, but I still thank him many times each year. The fire, along with a number of other traumatic events, led to me losing my speech. For months I was silent, and then, well, I croaked, spat, stamped, pulled faces, bent double, and burnt my face red. The speech had returned and with it a stutter, a horrendous and fierce nemesis that was about to ruin my childhood. They called me 'Tommy Gun' because I said 'bbbbbbbbb'. They called me 'Sizzler' for when I tried to say an 's' I hissed like a snake. They called me a freak. I withdrew as it was easier to say nothing. Why give them their fun as I struggled to say any words? Aged eight I was packed off to the children's hospital in Heswell. Ex-Hurricane Ringo Starr had been a patient there as a child and had donated a boat that sat in the grounds. I played pirates on a Hurricanes boat, though I never knew it then. They taught me to speak through singing. I sang every sentence with ease, for you cannot stutter when you sing unless you mean to do it. But the stutter was waiting, and when I spoke it was there again. I withdrew once more.

I was twelve when my world changed, and funnily enough it was an ex-Beatle who started it all – Tommy Moore, who had sat in with The Beatles on drums during their tour of Scotland in 1960 as well as a number of local gigs. Most important however, he was a pal of my father and a good family friend. I liked him a lot, and loved listening to him. One day he was telling me about The Beatles (I was bored, they did not interest me – I was only twelve). He then mentioned a man named Rory Storm, telling me how he had a terrible stutter, but sang in a band. I was amazed. Here was a guy like me but he was singing to many people. How could he have done this? I was now hooked, asking Tommy everything about Rory. I read all that I could about him and his band called The Hurricanes. He amazed me, thrilled me, and spurred me on. From then it was 'If Rory could do it, I can do it.' He became my idol; I looked up to him so much.

Within a year I was acting in school plays – me on a stage! The stutter was still there, but it was improving. I had also made a discovery: I had wit, a wit that made people laugh and made me popular. It was a great defence against anyone who felt the need to insult me, and I tended to

Rory Storm. (Courtesy of Iris Caldwell)

come out the best when I used my wit to bring down a would-be offender. Some people still thought I was nuts and a freak, but I cared nothing about that for I had found confidence, and it felt good. I went on to learn the guitar, and played bass in a band – not the greatest bass player, but up there doing it like Rory. My stutter eased as my confidence grew, and by my mid-twenties it was all but gone. It still raises its head at times, but just for a few words, and I sometimes sing a line when I feel the need. But on the whole it is gone.

It has been an absolute pleasure to research these lads. I have met many wonderful people along the way and made many good friends in the process. I have been privileged to meet with ex-band members, their families, and their friends. Throughout the meetings it became clear that everyone was protective of these guys, who are clearly still loved very much. The whole experience has bounced me from high fits of laughter to having to get a grip of my emotions. But that is their story: fun and the sorrow go together. Writing about these boys has been an overwhelming journey that I will treasure forever. My intentions were to produce and preserve The Hurricanes' story so as to keep their memory flowing. But this book will only go a tiny way towards doing that, for these guys are unforgettable.

Rory Storm/Alan Caldwell changed my life. Through having him as an icon and looking up to him, I changed, grew strong, and became confident. I owe him much and cannot tell him, but I can remember him, and I do with gratitude. Of course The Hurricanes became my favourite band, along with The Who and Madness (stop laughing, they are great).

The Hurricanes. (Courtesy of Walter Eymond)

They only had a handful of recordings, so most of my fandom was through reading about them, with the rest of the band becoming idols to me as well. Then, Rory's sister Iris found the 1960 tape of them performing at the Jive Hive in Crosby. It was released as a CD, and we now had a full set of their performance, along with four home recordings – total bliss. We also have people sharing their memories of the lads, and hardly a bad word has ever been spoken or written about them. How many people can claim that? They say that Alan/Rory never cured his stutter. Well he cured mine.

'Ladies and Gentlemen. Put your hands together and show your appreciation for Rory Storm and The Hurricanes.'

Acknowledgements

I would like to thank the following people for their invaluable input and for providing so many stories for this book: Iris Caldwell, Walter Eymond, Ted Kingsize Taylor, Jimmy Tushingham, and Dave Jamo Jamieson. I would also like to thank them for their help and time spent talking me through events and facts. Thank you to the families of the band members, who have been so good with me, and so patient, as I asked question after question. Thanks to Jean Beach, Ronnie Blackwell, and Sue Hogan for her constant support. Sam Hogan, Julie Sudbury, Bob Hardy for allowing his interview with Johnny guitar to be reproduced here. Carl Wharton, Eddie Porter, Faron Ruffley and Alix Watson. Mike Callan, Mikey Rogers, Amy Brookes, Ged Fagan, Peter Paetzold and Matthias Fraider for being my wonderful guides in Hamburg, Gibson and Tina Kemp, Pothos for being a huge Hurricanes fan, Kathleen Faulkner, Dave May, Martin and Lynne Jones, David Bedford, Sam Leach for the use of information from his book *The Rocking City: The Explosive Birth of the Beatles*, Wallasey Central Reference Library, *The Liverpool Echo* archives, The Beatle Forum, and a huge thank you to the very talented Gaz Wato for the book cover design, the fantastic drawing of Rory Storm, and for his constant egging me on to write. Also to thirteen-year-old Gary Watson, the up-and-coming Liverpool actor who inspires and amazes me. He has the talent and ability to take on such a demanding role as Rory Storm when age will allow him.

All photographs within this book carry details of ownership beneath them. Any that are not marked this way are ownership and copyright of the author.